ALICE, GRAND DUCHE
PRINCESS OI
GREAT BRITAIN AND

LETTERS

TO HER MAJESTY THE QUEEN

WITH A MEMOIR

BY H.R.H. PRINCESS CHRISTIAN

Volume I

Elibron Classics
www.elibron.com

Elibron Classics series.

© 2005 Adamant Media Corporation.

ISBN 1-4021-7430-6 (paperback)
ISBN 1-4021-2466-X (hardcover)

This Elibron Classics Replica Edition is an unabridged facsimile
of the edition published in 1885 by Bernhard Tauchnitz,
Leipzig.

COLLECTION

OF

BRITISH AUTHORS

TAUCHNITZ EDITION.

VOL. 2348.

ALICE, GRAND DUCHESS OF HESSE

IN TWO VOLUMES.

VOL. 1.

LEIPZIG: BERNHARD TAUCHNITZ.

PARIS: C. REINWALD, 15, RUE DES SAINTS PÈRES.

PARIS: THE GALIGNANI LIBRARY, 224, RUE DE RIVOLI,
AND AT NICE, 15, QUAI MASSENA.

COLLECTION

OF

BRITISH AUTHORS

TAUCHNITZ EDITION.

VOL. 2348.

ALICE, GRAND DUCHESS OF HESSE.

IN TWO VOLUMES.—VOL. I.

TAUCHNITZ EDITION.

LEAVES FROM THE JOURNAL OF OUR LIFE IN THE
    HIGHLANDS FROM 1848 TO 1861 . . . . . . 1 vol.
MORE LEAVES FROM THE JOURNAL OF A LIFE IN
    THE HIGHLANDS FROM 1862 TO 1882 . . . . 1 vol.

H R H The Princess Alice

1860

Leipzig Bernhard Tauchnitz

ALICE

GRAND DUCHESS OF HESSE

PRINCESS

OF

GREAT BRITAIN AND IRELAND

LETTERS TO HER MAJESTY THE QUEEN.

WITH

A MEMOIR BY H.R.H. PRINCESS CHRISTIAN.

COPYRIGHT EDITION.

IN TWO VOLUMES.—VOL. I.

WITH PORTRAIT.

LEIPZIG

BERNHARD TAUCHNITZ

1885.

PREFACE.

IN PUBLISHING a new and revised edition of my dear Sister's Letters, some extracts from my Mother's Journal have been added, and the Memoir translated from the German has been replaced by a short biographical sketch written by myself, in which I have tried to tell the story of my dear Sister's life as simply as I could, and to picture her as she was, the loving Daughter and Sister, the devoted Wife and Mother, and a perfect, true Woman.

It would have been premature and out of place to attempt anything like a complete picture of a character so many-sided, or of my Sister's ideas on the affairs of Europe, in which she took the deepest interest, and on which she formed opinions remarkable for breadth and sagacity of view. The domestic side of her nature might alone for the present be freely dealt with. There was no thought at first of making these letters public, but they were found to be so beautiful, and to be so true an expression of what my Sister really was, that, in compliance with the request of the Grand Duke her husband, they were allowed to be translated into German and published, so that her subjects might see in them how great reason they had to love her whom they had lost.

The letters in their original form are now given to the English public, and I am sure that all who read them will feel thankful to my Mother for thus granting them a closer insight into my dear Sister's beautiful and unselfish life.

They will see in them also, with satisfaction, how devoted she was to the land of her birth,— how her heart ever turned to it with reverence and affection as the country which had done and was doing for liberty and the advancement of mankind more than any other country in the world. How deep was her feeling in this respect was destified by a request, which she made to her husband in anticipation of her death, that an English flag might be laid upon her coffin; accompanying the wish with a modest expression of a hope, that no one in the land of her adoption could take umbrage at her desire to be borne to her rest with the old English colours above her.

I feel confident that the perusal of these letters must deepen the love and admiration which has always been felt for my beloved Sister in this country, where she ever thanked God that her childhood and youth had been tended with a wise love, that had fostered and developed all those qualities and tastes which she most valued and strove to cultivate in her later years.

HELENA.

CUMBERLAND LODGE:
January 1885.

CONTENTS

OF VOLUME I.

———

1866.

1867.

MEMOIR OF PRINCESS ALICE.

MEMOIR OF PRINCESS ALICE.

BY HER SISTER

PRINCESS CHRISTIAN.

———

On the 25th of April, 1843, at Buckingham Palace, a second daughter and third child was born to the Queen and Prince Consort — Alice Maud Mary—who ever since has been known and loved in the country of her birth as "Princess Alice." She was christened on the 2nd of June. The Queen, in a letter written at the time to her uncle the King of the Belgians, describes the ceremony as having been "very imposing," and mentions that "little Alice behaved extremely well."

Her childhood was, like that of all her brothers and sisters, a very happy one. Indeed, few children can ever have been more blessed in their home life. "When she was a year old, her father mentions her as the 'beauty of the family, and an extraordinarily good and merry child,' and her mother adds, 'she was a very vain little person.'"

She had the brightest, happiest nature, and was a great favourite with all around her.

At the age of two years, the Queen mentions Princess Alice in her Journal as follows:

"Alice is really a treasure, the dearest, sweetest, funniest little pet I ever saw; so little, and so fat, and so active and dear and gentle, with such a funny long little face, and such a sweet little voice."

And, writing again a year later, the Queen says:

"Dear little Alice comes to me every morning while I am dressing, and she really is the dearest little bijou I ever saw, and our very great pet. She has such little independent, winning ways, she talks so plain and says so dearly, 'Let me kiss you, dear mama.'"

The education and training, both mental and bodily, of their children, was an object of unceasing solicitude to the Queen and the Prince Consort, who themselves chose with the utmost care those persons who, under them, were to carry out their plans. The Queen, in a memorandum dated the 4th of March, 1844, writes as follows: "The greatest maxim of all is, that the children should be brought up as simply and in as domestic a way as possible, that (not interfering with their lessons) they should be as much as possible with their parents, and learn to place their greatest confidence in them in all things."

On leaving the nursery the children were entrusted to the care of an English governess and of a German and a French governess. These again were under a lady superintendent. * It was the governesses who directed the children's studies, accompanied them in their walks, and watched over them in their playtime. The Queen and the Prince Consort were kept informed of the minutest details of their education by these ladies, in whom they had the utmost confidence, and who were allowed at all times direct communication with them.

* Lady Lyttelton from 1842 to 1851; and then Lady Caroline Barrington, who remained with the Royal Family till her death.

Princess Alice learnt with great facility, and showed great talent for music and drawing. "Her copy-books were always neatness itself, and she wrote a very pretty hand." "Fresh, blooming, and healthy, escaping most of the illnesses of childhood. Cheerful, merry, full of fun and mischief."

Such are her eldest sister's words when mentioning her as a child.

She excelled in skating and gymnastics, and was especially devoted to riding. At the age of four the Queen writes of her as follows:

"November 12, 1847.

"The children rode on the rocking-horse with great delight, and Alice really distinguished herself by riding upon it and making it go very high, and sitting on one side without any pommel or stirrup, and without being held on."

I myself well remember her devotion as a child to a silver *bonbonnière* in the shape of a horse's head, in which she kept a piece of the tail and mane of her favourite horse, and used to put it under her pillow when she went to bed at night.

Her romps and games with her brothers were what she particularly loved; and, though so fearless and bold, she was full of gentleness, kindness of heart, and consideration for others.

It was the custom among the Royal Children to celebrate in some way or other all anniversaries in the family, often preparing charming surprises for their parents. In the little theatrical pieces which they performed, Princess Alice never failed to distinguish herself. Her rendering of the part of "Joad the High Priest" in Racine's *Athalie* was most remarkable.

The following account of the Princess's acting in Racine's piece is from the Queen's own Journal:

"February 10, 1852.

"At six the children performed their fragment from *Athalie*. Vicky,* 'Athalie;' Alice, 'Joad the High Priest' and 'Josabeth' (she acted two characters); 'Agar, *suivante* of Athalie,' Lenchen;** 'Joas,' Affie;*** 'Abner, *un officier,*' Bertie;†

---

* Princess Royal.   ** Princess Helena.
*** Prince Alfred,   † Prince of Wales.

2 *

'Zacharie, the boy of Josabeth,' Louise. The dresses were extremely pretty and simple and graceful. Vicky looked extremely well, and spoke and acted her long and difficult part (the celebrated scene describing her dream, which is Rachel's great part) really admirably, with immense expression and dignity, and with the true French emphasis, which indeed they all did. She looked very well, Lenchen lovely, and Affie beautiful in his little white tunic-robe and long hair. Little Zacharie was dressed just alike. Alice was *méconnaissable* as the priest with a white beard and hair, and very handsome in her second character: she acted beautifully; Affie very nicely; Bertie very well. He and Alice appeared in the first scene; the curtain then dropped to enable Alice to change her dress, and the music from Mendelssohn's *Athalie* was played. The scenery used was that from *Julius Cæsar*.

"Mama and Lady Anna Maria,* the Ladies, Stockmar, Phipps, and children, Colonel Grey and Sybil, Lady Caroline and daughter, and Mr. Wellesley were there.

"My beloved Albert was much pleased and surprised, for he had no idea of it."

* Lady Anna Maria Dawson, Lady in Waiting to the Duchess of Kent.

Baroness Bunsen in her *Mémoires* of her husband also gives a description of one of these per-
formances, which took place on the anniversary of
the Queen and Prince Consort's wedding day,
February 10, 1854. On this occasion a tableau of
the Four Seasons had been arranged by the Royal
Children as a surprise for their parents.

"First appeared Princess Alice as the Spring,
scattering flowers, and reciting verses, which were
taken from Thomson's *Seasons;* she moved grace-
fully, and spoke in a distinct and pleasing manner
with excellent modulation, and a tone of voice sweet
and penetrating like that of the Queen."*

An extract from the Queen's Journal on this
subject will be read with interest:

"At near six we went over with the whole party
to the Rubens Room, where the children had kindly
arranged a charming surprise for us. The room
was entirely darkened. There were five tableaux.
Four of these represented the Seasons. 1. Alice as
Spring recited some very pretty verses from Thomson's

* Bunsen's *Life*, II. 328.

Seasons. 2. Vicky as Summer, with dear little Arthur asleep near some sheaves; she also recited verses. 3. Affie as Bacchus, representing Autumn, also reciting verses. 4. Bertie with a long icicled beard and snowy cloak, and Louise in a sort of Russian dress sitting before a fire, as Winter: this was the prettiest almost. Bertie also recited some verses: all were taken and adapted from Thomson's *Seasons*. The fifth and last tableau combined the four others as they had each been separately represented, and in the clouds at the back stood dear little Lenchen and recited, as the spirit of the Empress Helena, very pretty verses written on the occasion by Mr. Martin Tupper. Lenchen spoke beautifully, and looked lovely. The scenery was admirably adapted to each tableau; appropriate music was played between each. The children spoke well (Alice beautifully), and looked very pretty. All were so anxious to do their best. Mr. Corbould,* Miss Hildyard,** and Mr. Gibbs*** had the merit of the whole arrangement.

"We were all delighted."

As years went on, her intellectual faculties and

---

* The Princes and Princesses' drawing-master.
** Princesses' English governess.
*** Prince of Wales's and Prince Alfred's tutor.

those rarer qualities of her character became more and more apparent; above all, a wonderful sweetness of disposition which endeared her to all around. She had a great power of observation and a remarkable gift of making herself attractive to others.

With all this she continued merry, full of fun and mischief, and always a great favourite with her brothers and sisters.

It is often maintained that none but those who live in comparative retirement really know the blessings of a home life. Certainly the contrary was proved in this royal English family, and none knew better how to appreciate this than Princess Alice. The happy daily intercourse with her parents; the many walks, drives, journeys with them and her brothers and sisters; the various occupations and amusements, all watched over and shared in by the Queen and the Prince Consort, make up the sum of a most perfectly happy childhood and youth. Her adoration for her father became the one leading star through all her life; it influenced her every thought and action, and to the end of her short stay on earth she strove to act up to what he would

have thought right. He was her highest ideal of
all that was perfect, beautiful, and good, and even
on her deathbed his loved name was the last she
ever uttered.

After the Princess Royal's marriage* Princess
Alice had to assume the position of eldest daughter
in the house, and this brought with it more responsibilities and more duties. She had hitherto
shared all joys and sorrows, all studies and recrea-
tions, with her sister. Now her intercourse with her
parents became a much more intimate one, and,
under the guidance of her father, she soon showed
her appreciation of all that was purest and noblest
in art, whether in painting or in music. The Prince
Consort strove at all times to imbue his children
with that honesty and thoroughness of purpose without which "it was impossible to fill one's position
in life happily, worthily, and with dignity."**

The Revolution of 1848—1849, the Crimean
War, and other political disturbances throughout

---

* Princess Royal was married on the 25th of January,
1858, to Prince Frederick William of Prussia.

** Baron Stockmar.

Europe, happening as they did at a time when the Princess was just old enough to appreciate their importance, laid the foundation of that keen interest and clear understanding she showed later in all political events.

Princess Alice's Confirmation took place on the 21st of April, 1859. She had been prepared for it by the Dean of Windsor (the Honourable and Very Reverend G. Wellesley). The Prince Consort had also read with her every evening for the previous few months. The following extract from the Queen's own Journal gives an account of those eventful days:

"April 20, 1859.

"At a quarter past four dear Alice's examination took place by the Dean in the presence of ourselves, the Archbishop, and Miss Hildyard. It lasted more than half an hour in her own room. She answered extremely well, without any hesitation or agitation, better than either of the others, and seemed so relieved when it was over, as she said she was so frightened. She behaved admirably."

"April 21.

"We gave dear Alice a pretty Prayer Book. At twelve all was ready. The two little girls and Arthur were present. Albert went to fetch dear Alice. She looked very nice and pretty in a muslin dress trimmed with lace over white silk, her pearl necklace her only ornament. Albert led her into the chapel; Ernest Coburg, me; George, Mama. We two and the three children stood on one side; Ernest, Mama, &c., opposite. Music very fine, the whole very moving, reminding me so much of dear Vicky, three years ago.* Dear Alice seemed much moved when we came out and kissed her.

"We went to the 'King's rooms,' where were all Alice's presents.

"We talked with the company, including Lord Clarendon, who hoped things were coming right. Vain hope! At that very moment Albert was called out by Lord Derby, whose face told nothing but *bad news*. He soon returned with the distressing news that Austria had sent a summons to Sardinia to disarm, giving them three days' time to answer, at the end of which time the Austrians would march on Turin. Terribly distressed and *bouleversée* on such a day and at such a moment."

* Princess Royal's Confirmation, which took place at Windsor, the 20th of March, 1856.

"April 22.

"Dear Alice breakfasted with us. We took the Sacrament with her, Ernest, Lady Gainsborough, Miss Hildyard, and Fräulein Bauer. Immediately after it we walked out with Alice, and found it very hot and beautiful, all so green, birds singing beautifully.

"We and all the children attended evening service."

"April 25.

"To-day is our dear and sweet Alice's sixteenth birth-day! I can hardly believe it possible. She is a great treasure and a child who only is a comfort and pleasure to us. May God leave her long with us, and may she ever be blessed, preserved, and protected! We wished one another warmly joy. Put on a new dress. When dressed we went to fetch our dear Alice, gave her a nosegay, and took her with all the children to the breakfast room."

It was in June 1860 that Princess Alice first made the acquaintance of her future husband. The Queen and Prince Consort always received many guests at Windsor Castle during the Ascot race week, and this year amongst others were Prince Louis and Prince Henry of Hesse.

It soon became evident to her parents that the
Princess and Prince Louis had formed a "mutual
liking for one another," and they had but little
doubt "that it would lead to further advances from
the young gentleman's family." Even that little
doubt was soon removed, and Prince Louis of Hesse
returned to Windsor Castle during the month of
November 1860.

On the 30th of November the Queen wrote as
follows in her Diary:

". . . After dinner, whilst talking to the gentlemen, I perceived Alice and Louis talking before
the fireplace more earnestly than usual, and when I
passed to go to the other room, both came up to
me, and Alice in much agitation said he had proposed to her, and he begged for my blessing. I
could only squeeze his hand and say 'Certainly,'
and that we would see him in our room later. Got
through the evening as well as we could. Alice
came to our room . . . agitated, but quiet. . . .
Albert sent for Louis to his room; he went first to
him and then called Alice and me in. . . . Louis
has a warm noble heart. We embraced our dear
Alice, and praised her much to him. He pressed

and kissed my hand, and I embraced him. After talking a little, we parted; a most touching, and to me most sacred, moment."

The marriage gave general satisfaction, and from being one entirely of mutual affection * there was every reason to think that a very bright and happy future was in store for the Princess.

March of 1861 brought the first great sorrow to the bright and happy home. The Duchess of Kent, the beloved mother and grandmother, was taken to her rest. She had been ailing for some time, but her condition had become much more serious since the commencement of the year, and though she was as full of life and interest as ever, and apparently unchanged, all those near her felt that her state was most precarious.

On the 16th of March, 1861, the Duchess of Kent gently breathed her last. The Queen and Prince Consort and Princess Alice were with her, and it was then that the young Princess first showed

---

* "Alice and Louis are as happy as mortals can be, and I need scarcely say this makes my heart as a father glad."—*Prince Consort's Letter to the Crown Princess.*

that wonderfully tender sympathy, and that perfect unselfishness of her nature, which but a few months later, when a far bitterer sorrow fell on her family, proved the comfort and solace of her broken-hearted mother.

The Queen writes in her Diary at that time:

"Dear good Alice was full of intense feeling, tenderness and distress for me." And again: "Good Alice was with us through all."

In the spring the Queen announced to Parliament Princess Alice's engagement; and when, later on, "the Princess's settlement of a dowry of 30,000*l.* with an annuity of 6,000*l.* was brought before the House of Commons, it was voted unanimously." * Her father, writing on this subject to Baron Stockmar, mentions, that as the Princess's income would not be a large one, she "would not be able to do great things with it."

Prince Louis of Hesse paid several visits to England during the year—one of the last being to the Highlands. Balmoral had ever been peculiarly

* *Prince Consort's Life.* Sir Theodore Martin.

dear to the Princess, and in her letters to the
Queen after her marriage she gives constant proof
of her love for her Scotch home.

On the return of the Court to Windsor Castle,
the preparations for the Princess's marriage were
being carried rapidly forward, her father himself
directing and settling all. It was whilst engaged
on these that he was taken ill with typhoid fever,
and died on the 14th of December, 1861.

The light and sunshine seemed to have gone
out of that hitherto so happy home. Though utterly
crushed by the loss of the father whom she so adored,
all thought of herself was put aside, and she only
lived for her mother. What she was to her in those
first terrible weeks is well known; and it was at that
time that an article appeared in the *Times*, from
which the following extract is taken:

"It is impossible to speak too highly of the
strength of mind and self-sacrifice shown by Princess
Alice during these dreadful days. Her Royal Highness has certainly understood that it was her duty
to be the help and support of her mother in her
great sorrow, and it was in a great measure due to

her that the Queen has been able to bear with
such wonderful resignation the irreparable loss that
so suddenly and terribly befell her."

In every way in her power the Princess strove to
guard her mother from all that was painful, to help
her over all that was unavoidable. Since her father's
death she had developed a force of character, combined with tact and judgment, truly admirable, settling and arranging everything for the Queen with
Ministers and officials, and sustaining her mother
by her own firmness and skilfully ministered sympathy; and when it was decided, at the urgent desire of the King of the Belgians, that the Queen
must leave Windsor for Osborne but a few days
after the Prince's death, it was the Princess's gentle
influence which induced her mother to make that
great sacrifice. "She also gained at this time that
practical knowledge for organising, and the desire
for constant occupation, which in her public as in
her private life became a part of herself." *

Princess Alice's marriage took place at Osborne
on the 1st of July, 1862. The following most touch-

---

* By the Grand Duchess of Baden.

ing accounts of the wedding and the days after it, from the Queen's own Journal, will be read with the deepest interest.

"July 1, 1862.

"A very bad night, very little sleep, and towards morning heard the knocking for the arrangements for the sad marriage. When dear Alice got up and came and kissed me I gave her my blessing and a Prayer Book, like the one dear mama gave me the day of our happy marriage, and another very pretty book. Got up a little earlier, and breakfasted with dear Alice. . . . Went with Colonel Biddulph to look at the dining-room arranged as a chapel, with the altar just under our dear family picture. A dark blue velvet cloth and cushions, and chairs covered with dark blue cloth, rails in a circular form, like at our blessed wedding and Vicky's; the furniture taken out of the room. Then the breakfast for the Royal personages in the Council Room, where our marriage picture was placed (the deer-stalking one had been taken away for the Exhibition, and I had this brought from Windsor on purpose).

"Took a very short drive with Lenchen, and then sent for dear Louis, who was much overcome when I kissed him and wished him joy; and so was I. Dear Alice was dressed by a little before one.

She looked lovely in her bridal attire. Unlike Vicky she had no train, and had a berthe and half-long sleeves. The deep flounce of Honiton lace and the veil to correspond were chosen by my beloved angel, he having seen last spring the designs and ordered a new one to be made, as that first sent was "so unmeaning." Ever his precious taste!

"Darling Alice had her order on, the beautiful opal cross and brooches of her adored papa, and Bertie's bracelet and the one with our pictures in it. She looked most lovely, with rather a full wreath of orange flowers and myrtle. The dress of crystalline silk, no more flowers but round the bottom of the dress. The four bridesmaids, our three girls and Anna,* were in sprigged net over white, with grey silk ribbon trimming. The time came. I, in my sad cap, as dear Baby calls it—most sad on such a day—went down with our four boys, Bertie and Affie leading me. It was dreadful; and yet I felt him very near. No one in the room except the Archbishop of York (the Archbishop of Canterbury not being strong enough), the Dean, and Mr. Prothero. Felt very nervous when I heard the doors open and the different people one after another walk in, though no one could see me, for I sat the whole time in an

---

* Prince Louis' sister.

arm-chair near the altar, and Bertie and Affie stood close to my right and hid me; the little boys to my left. The parents and Wilhelm* stood opposite to me, and the Augustuses** and Nemours next to them. Another painful pause and Louis came in, conducted by Lord Sidney, and followed by Heinrich.*** Again a still more painful pause, and in complete silence in came the dear dear bride on her uncle's arm, followed by her bridesmaids—a touching sight—and the service began. The Archbishop read most impressively, solemnly. Dear Alice answered sweetly, distinctly, and in her harmonious voice, full of dignity and self-possession. Louis answered very distinctly and plainly. I restrained my tears (poor dear Affie cried terribly all through) till the words which I never could bear, and which have been fulfilled in an earthly sense, "till death us do part," were pronounced, and then I had a violent struggle to prevent a complete outburst. I feel he is near me as ever, and his beloved picture† where he stretches out his hand as though he blessed us.

* Prince William of Hesse.
** Prince and Princess Augustus of Saxe-Coburg and Gotha.
*** Prince Henry of Hesse.
† Family picture by Winterhalter. The altar was arranged underneath the picture.

"All over! Dearest Alice, who was wonderfully calm, embraced *me*, who was *all* she had, while Louis embraced his parents, who were much affected. Then I embraced dear Louis and his parents. I then left the room, shook Ernest's* hand and kissed him, and dearest Feodore** came and embraced me. When all had left I got up and went as I had come, and took and pressed the Archbishop's hand as I passed him, the tears rolling down his cheeks. Went at once with the boys to the Horn Room, where I cried bitterly, and clasped dear Affie in my arms, who sobbed very much, and was terribly overcome; the little boys too. Alice and Louis then came in, and Prince and Princess Charles, who were very much upset, and Prince Charles so kind, saying he felt so much for me. Good dear Fritz*** came to kiss me, and was very much moved. The Dean then arrived with the three registers, which we signed, and which took a long time; after which the young couple left the room. Heinrich, Wilhelm, and Anna† as well as the other bridesmaids, came in also. Darling Baby cried very much. Then in succession the Cambridges, most feeling, and other

---

  * Duke of Saxe-Coburg and Gotha.
 ** Princess Hohenlohe Langenburg.
*** Crown Prince of Prussia.
  † Prince Louis' two brothers and sister.

Princes, came in, including Nemours. I took leave of all, and then went upstairs, followed by the dear young couple, who lunched with me and Baby in the schoolroom, all the others lunching below.

"Mr. Thomas made a slight sketch of Alice in her dress, and then she went into her dear papa's room and changed, putting on a white muslin de soie. Her calmness and composure continued. They both went over to wish the Prince and Princess good-bye, who then came with their children to wish me good-bye, after which they all left. Ernest went with them to town, to return on Thursday. Dear Alice and Louis came to me, and I talked a little to her. . . . At five she put on her white tulle bonnet with orange flowers, and I took leave of her, and blessed them both, and saw them from the stairs drive off to St. Clare—Jane Churchill, General Seymour, and Baron Westerweller following them."

"July 3, 1862.

"At twenty minutes to three started with Feodore, the two girls, Bertie, the Duchess of Athole, and Mademoiselle de Schenck, for St. Clare,* going a long way round to avoid Ryde, and to arrive there

* Villa near Ryde belonging to Colonel and Lady Catherine Harcourt.

a little before six. Most strange it seemed to see
dear Alice and Louis and their people at the door.
But oh! to come alone, without my own blessed one,
the incredibility of which, when I think of so many
years—of last year—was too dreadful, and gave all
a sad, sad tinge. Dear Alice had rather a cold, but
seemed well and happy, very quiet and *posée*, but
yet sad too. They gave us tea. We left a little
before seven."

"July 4.

"Went to Alice and Louis's rooms. At half-past
seven o'clock they arrived; took them to their room
—the same Vicky had, and Prince and Princess
Charles had, but they have been fresh done up.
New carpets with orange flowers and wreaths of
flowers, and their cyphers. They dined with me,
and are very nice together."

"July 5.

"After luncheon gave dear Louis the Garter. Of
course only put it over his shoulder. He was very
much pleased, and said, 'Ich hoffe ich werde mich
immer würdig zeigen.' "*

---

* "I hope I shall ever prove myself worthy of it."

"July 6.

"Feodore dined with me, and after it the others came up. Bertie and Affie went to play billiards, and Louis remained with us. Alice read aloud the *Lady of Shalot.*"

"July 7, 1862.

"Alice came over to me and played a few of our chapel hymns. Alice drove me, and it again turned showery—Louis and the others riding. Went with Alice to her room; she and Louis dined with me. After dinner the boys went down to play at billiards again. Took Alice to her room, being her last night, and she began to cry bitterly; and I strove to cheer her by the prospect of an early return, but she said, 'It is my home,' and its being so sad made no difference in it, she loved it so much: she loved me, poor dear child!"

"July 8, 1862.

"Went out with Alice and Louis, first walking to play with the monkey, and then driving in little Sardinian pony carriage, Louis sitting behind. Alice received an immense number of pretty presents from all the household, chiefly ornaments for the table, china, &c.—really beautiful things. She and Louis came over to my room, and while she was seeing Dr. Becker * in the next room, Louis remained with me, and talked very sensibly of Alice's health, &c. I feel quite satisfied as to her happiness; nothing can be nicer than their tone together, or more truly satisfied and happy, though Alice is serious; but I feel anxious about her health, she is grown very thin again. Louis is extremely unselfish, and made so little fuss about keeping her to himself, and is very affectionate to me; and Alice praises him so much, finds him so sensible, not narrow-minded or prejudiced.

"Baby and Leopold to luncheon. Soon after Alice again came to me, and I afterwards went over to her room and saw her put her things on, and at half-past four took her over to our side and here had to take leave. She was very much overcome, but I tried to bear up as much as I could and not to cry too violently. Blessed her, and felt (D. V.) we should meet again at the end of October.

"Louis was excessively upset. I told him I gave Alice to him in perfect confidence. I joined their hands again, and embraced them, and then they left, and I felt *all alone.*"

---

* Princess Alice's private secretary, who had formerly been private secretary and librarian to the Prince Consort.

On the 8th of July the Princess and her husband left for her new home. Many were the earnest prayers, and many were the loving wishes, that accompanied her on her leaving her English home— that home to which she clung even more passionately as years went on.

"Dear to us all by those calm earnest eyes,
    And early thought upon that fair young brow;
    Dearer for that where grief was heaviest, thou
Wert sunshine, till He passed where suns shall rise
And set no more: thou, in affection wise
    And strong, wert strength to Her who even but now
    In the soft accents of thy bridal vow
Heard music of her own heart's memories.

  "Too full of love to own a thought of pride
Is now thy gentle bosom; so 'tis best:
    Yet noble is thy choice, O English bride!
And England hails the bridegroom and the guest
    A friend—a friend well loved by him who died.
He blessed your troth; your wedlock shall be blessed."

Punch.

July 1862.

MARRIED LIFE.

THE young married couple met with a most enthusiastic reception on their arrival at Darmstadt. From far and near the people had flocked together to do honour to their young Prince's bride. The Princess created the very best impression, and all were captivated by her great simplicity and grace, and at the same time by the wonderful dignity of her demeanour.

The first few weeks after their arrival were fully occupied by the official duties of their position. In the autumn the Princess had the joy of meeting her mother and several of her brothers and sisters, who had come to Germany (to Rheinhardsbrunn in Thuringia, a shooting castle of the Duke of Coburg's) for a few weeks.

Prince and Princess Louis decided to come to England at the beginning of the winter and spend some months with the Queen. This they did, and on Easter Sunday, the 5th of April, 1863, a little daughter* was born to the Prince and Princess at Windsor Castle, and was christened there a few weeks later.

Early in the summer they returned to Germany, spending the hottest months at Kranichstein, a shooting castle of the Grand Duke's near Darmstadt, beautifully situated among large beech woods. Here the Princess lived a most quiet, happy life, much occupied with ideas and plans of how she could best prove her love and interest for her adopted country and its people.

"The Congress" of crowned heads and princes of Germany (which took place at Frankfort in August 1863 under the auspices of Austria, the King of Prussia declining to be present) called forth afresh the Princess's interest in politics. Her letters of that time show how keenly she entered into the great questions which were then stirring Germany to its very core—foremost among them the Schles-

* Victoria, married, April 30, 1884, to Prince Louis of Battenberg.

wig-Holstein question, which soon became one of European importance, and out of which sprang the war of 1866.

A second daughter* was born at Darmstadt on the 1st of November, 1864. During that and the previous years the Princess superintended the building of her own palace, which she had planned herself. She had hitherto lived in a very small house adjoining the palace of her parents-in-law, Prince and Princess Charles of Hesse, and it was felt to be impossible, with an increasing family, for her and the Prince to continue living there; besides, they were quite unable to receive the society of Darmstadt—in fact, to fulfil the social duties of their position.

Much of the Princess's time was always taken up in organising and carrying out various schemes for the good and welfare of the people at Darmstadt, and in Hesse generally. This was no easy task, for she met with many difficulties and had to combat with many prejudices. The mere fact of

* Elizabeth, married, June 1884, to the Grand Duke Sergius of Russia.

her being an Englishwoman with broad and liberal views excited suspicion in a certain set. She felt this very keenly from the first, but more so as time went on. Yet the great love and respect universally felt for her in her new home, deeply appreciated by her, encouraged her to persevere in her efforts.

Some time in each year was spent in England with the Queen, and though so thoroughly happy in her husband's country, each return to the old home only strengthened the Princess's passionate attachment to it.

The death of the King of the Belgians, December 1865, who had been the kindest and tenderest of uncles, was a great grief to the Princess, who felt deeply what an irreparable loss the death of this wise, devoted friend and counsellor would be to the Queen.

The year 1866 was an eventful one for Germany To the Princess it brought alike joys and sorrows, and, great as were the anxieties through which she had to pass, she felt in the end she had also much cause for thankfulness.

In the spring of the year a bazaar which she had herself arranged in her "new palace" took place with the most satisfactory results. This undertaking was for the purpose of raising funds to found an Idiot Asylum in Darmstadt. She had previously attended some lectures on the subject; and knowing the want of such an institution, she determined to found one herself.* At the outset she found herself much hampered by the different views prevailing on the subject; but with tact and patience, and with the help of kind friends, the Princess secured the success she so fully deserved. The Idiot Asylum founded by her is now doing its work nobly, and is carried out on the principles laid down by her. The proceeds of the bazaar amounted to 16,000 florins.

In June the war between Austria and Prussia broke out. The Princess was "such a true German" that she could not but be affected by it most nearly. It was a struggle between Germans and Germans, or, as she herself writes to her mother, of "brother

---

* See the Princess's letter of the 2nd of January, 1866.

against brother, and friend against friend." She knew but too well how Prince Louis and his country would suffer by it; she knew, too, that her husband must soon take the field with his division against Prussia. The Grand Duke of Hesse naturally went with the "Bund" (the German Confederation), and the Princess with her clear foresight saw how South Germany must suffer in the end through the struggle. The mere idea that her husband should stand opposed to the Crown Prince of Prussia (her brother-in-law) was bitter pain to her.

In the midst of this most trying time, the Princess gave birth to a third daughter on the 12th of July, 1866. By the merest chance Prince Louis had returned to Darmstadt for a few hours the very day the child was born, and she had the comfort of having him with her. On the 21st of July the Prussian General von Göben entered Darmstadt with his troops. The Princess, though barely recovered from her confinement, was aware of what took place, and was the comfort and stay of all at that time.

In August Prince Louis came home for a few days.

As soon as the Princess was sufficiently strong, she and her husband visited the wounded and endeavoured to organise means for their relief. On the 12th of September the baby Princess was christened at Darmstadt. The sponsors were the brigade Prince Louis commanded: "as a remembrance that he and they had stood in the field together for their first campaign, he asked these two regiments, officers and men, to stand sponsors to Baby, as she was born during that time, and they are delighted, but wish the child to have one of their names." *

The Princess had felt throughout the late war the necessity for a general and widespread organisation "for aid to the sick and wounded in times of war." A society had existed since 1865 in Hesse for this purpose, Prince and Princess Charles of Hesse being at its head. It had been established on the principle of the German Red Cross Society. Princess Alice, who was very much interested in the

---

* The Princess received the names Irène Louise Marie Anna.

movement, and in all that had to do with nursing, &c., resolved to found a "Ladies' Union," in which ladies and women of every rank and denomination should join. A committee was formed in 1867, consisting of seven ladies and four doctors, with Princess Alice at the head. Branch committees were to spring from it and be spread all over the country, to assist "the nursing and supporting of troops in times of war, and in times of peace to train nurses to assist other hospitals, and to help among the poor or to nurse the rich." *

At the same time that Princess Alice founded the "Ladies' Union for Aid to Sick and Wounded," she had turned her attention seriously to the subject of "the improvement of the condition of poor unmarried women and girls." Fräulein Louise Büchner, a distinguished philanthropist, proved a most efficient help to the Princess, and aided her in establishing a "Committee for the Encouragement of Female Industry."

The "Alice Bazaar" (a permanent one) was

---

* See the Princess's letter of the 21st of December, 1866.

founded on the 25th of November, 1867, "for the object of receiving and selling articles of needle-work, and for obtaining employment for women of all classes."

The year 1867 was not without its anxieties. There were rumours of war with France, which, however, passed off. The Princess, with her clear-sighted judgment, recognised that this could only be for a time. In a letter to her mother she writes as follows:

"Darmstadt: April 21, 1867.

". . . How I wish you may be right in *not* be-lieving in war. I always fear it is not Luxemburg, but the intense jealousy of the French nation, that they should not be the first on the Continent, and that Germany is becoming independent and power-ful against their will. Then, again, the Germans feel their new position, and assert their rights with more force because unanimous, and neither nation will choose to give in to the other.

"The war would be totally useless, and sow no end of dissension and hatred between the two neigh-bour countries, who, for their own good as for that of mankind, ought to live in peace and harmony with each other.

"We seem drifting back to the Middle Ages, as each question is pushed to the point of the sword. It is most sad. How dear Papa would have disapproved of much that has happened since 1862!"

The new Convention* entered into by the Grand Duchy of Hesse with Prussia was at first a great source of trouble to Prince Louis. He had every reason to fear that the Grand Duke, with his aversion to the new state of affairs, would never give a very hearty allegiance to it. Under these circumstances Prince Louis felt it incumbent on him to resign his command in the Hessian army, not wishing to appear in constant opposition to his uncle.

For some time there was great doubt whether the Grand Duke would agree to what was inevitable. The first condition under which the Prince considered it would be possible for him to retain the command was that he should have a Prussian officer at his side, and the Grand Duke had said he would rather lose his country than consent. However,

* Through which the Hessian army was placed under the King of Prussia's command.

4*

finally, to the surprise of all, he gave in to the Prince's wishes rather than lose his services.

During this year (1867) the strain of her life seemed to tell greatly on the Princess's health. She wrote in May to the Queen: "I am not up to very much. I don't always feel quite strong; but the change [to England] will do me good." A year or two before she had written: "From being always so well and strong, I feel a slight indisposition more than most people." As the years went on, this feeling of bodily weakness and the looking forward to change and rest recurred with more and more frequency.

The year 1868 brought great joy to the Prince and Princess and the whole country, in the birth of a son* and heir, on the 25th of November. During the autumn of the following year the Prince and Princess were for the first time separated for some months. Prince Louis accompanied the Crown Prince of Prussia on his tour to the East. Writing to the Queen at that time, the Princess says:** "I

---

* Ernst Ludwig.
** Darmstadt, October 3, 1869.

am very glad you approve of Louis' journey, which I know will be so useful and interesting to him, though it was not possible to attain this without parting from each other, which is of course no small trial to us who are so unaccustomed to being separated." The thought of what was best and what was most likely to benefit and fit the Prince for his future high position was ever her first thought, however great the personal sacrifice to herself. The Princess spent the time of her husband's absence with her sister the Crown Princess at Cannes. Prince Louis returned at Christmas, and the New Year saw them safe home at Darmstadt.

It was in the beginning of 1870 that Princess Alice became intimately acquainted with the great theological writer Frederick David Strauss. He was staying at Darmstadt at the time, and often spent some hours with the Princess reading aloud to her and conversing. This gave rise to a proposal, made by the Princess, that Strauss should make notes on Voltaire, whose works they had been discussing together, and then that he should read them to her, and to a select circle of friends, Mr. (now Sir Robert) Morier being amongst them. This plan, however, was never carried out, as Prince Louis was attacked by scarlet fever. The Princess then intimated to Strauss how glad she would be if he would come and read his lectures to her alone, provided he did not fear the risk of infection in coming to the palace. Strauss agreed to this most willingly. At the time he first took up the idea of writing these lectures on Voltaire for the Princess, he had hoped that when they were printed he might be allowed to dedicate them to her. He, however, quite gave up the idea when he had completed his book. He shrank from making the request, for fear it should place the Princess in a difficult position, owing to the views he held. After some discussion on the point, the Princess, with the full approbation of Prince Louis, accepted the dedication of the book in the terms in which it now stands published. Her intercourse with him has excited much comment, and been the cause of much misconception. The Princess at all times loved to gather around her people of distinction, of

whatever denomination. To discuss abstruse subjects with them, and become acquainted with their
opinions, was her great delight. She had a peculiar
talent in drawing others out, and an inclination to
enter, for the time at least, into their thoughts. It
was not strange, therefore, that she should have
been attracted by one so gifted as Strauss, nor was
it strange that, at a time when the Princess was
passing through a phase of mental struggle as to
her own religious views, this intercourse and real
friendship with Strauss should have exercised a
considerable influence on her opinions. It was,
however, but a phase, out of which she passed
triumphantly; not, alas, without much suffering to
herself, but only, as we now know from her own
letters, to become in the end more trustful and
strong in the most perfectly childlike faith.

She carried away from her own home that perfect fearlessness which has always been the true
reward of pure motives and true faith. The Princess had had occasion to learn how unjust public
clamour could be, even in a free country; but she
had also learnt the sacredness of the duty never to

join in such clamour, or to countenance it in any way, without a conscientious examination of the grounds on which it professed to rest.

In Germany the opinions of Strauss were looked upon with such dislike and distrust, that it required no small courage on the part of the Princess to make his acquaintance. To many people this would no doubt have proved a dangerous experiment, and even to her it was, as we know, a painful trial. As the true child of her father, she wished to prove everything, and to retain what was best; and she had her reward. What seemed a loss became to her a real gain, and in the future no page in her life will probably be read with deeper sympathy, no sacrifice that the Princess ever made will prove, it may be, a greater blessing to many "sick and wounded" in spirit, than her noble courage in facing a danger from which so many shrink, and the triumph of that childlike faith which in the end helped her to bear burdens which seemed almost too heavy to be borne.

Though in course of time she ceased to agree with Strauss in his views, she ever felt and acknow-

ledged his rare gifts and the perfect sincerity of
his nature.

In June 1870, France declared war against
Germany, and on the 1st of August Prince Louis
was ordered to the front with his division, which
formed part of the Second Army, commanded by
Prince Frederick Charles of Prussia.

The Princess had been much urged by her
sister, the Crown Princess, to pass the time of her
husband's absence with her; but she determined to
stay at Darmstadt. She considered that her parents-
in-law, who had all their sons in the war, had the
first claim upon her; and moreover, though she
knew all the comfort and advantage it would be
to her to be with her sister, it was a satisfaction
to her to be in her husband's home, nearer to him,
and where he would have wished her to stay. She
was living at Kranichstein with her children, and
drove in every morning early to Darmstadt to
attend the meeting of the "Society for Aid to the
Sick and Wounded," which she allowed to have its
"head-quarters" at her palace. She daily went to

the hospitals and ambulances, directing and organising the best means of relief, and bringing comfort and brightness wherever she went, proud to work like the wife of a German officer whose only thought during her husband's absence was to relieve as much as possible the misery and suffering of the wounded soldiers. "The Alice Society for Aid to Sick and Wounded" did grand work all this time. The Princess established a "dépôt" at her own palace of all hospital necessaries, and organised committees of ladies who served out refreshments day and night at the railway station to the wounded who were constantly passing through Darmstadt on their way home. She was indefatigable, never a thought given to herself, and though almost distracted with anxiety about the Prince, it was she who "kept others up," who kept her presence of mind, who directed, guided, advised, who comforted the bereaved, and gave hope to many ready to despair. But what tried her the most sorely was the heartrending. sight of the crowds of mothers, wives, sisters, pressing round her carriage after the first intelligence of a great battle: all came to her for news, and yet she was often unable to tell them anything but "that the loss had been enormous."

The strain on her health was intense, but she would not give in. In answer to one of her sisters writing to her at that time and begging her to spare herself, she said: "I must work only not to be able to think. I should go mad if I had to sit still and think;" and this, too, was shortly before her second boy's birth, which took place on the 6th of October.* After it, to help her recovery, she was persuaded by her parents-in-law to go for three weeks to her sister at Berlin. There is no doubt that the perpetual mental anxiety and the great physical strain of that terrible time told permanently on the Princess's health.

The christening of the little Prince had been deferred as long as possible in the hopes of Prince Louis being able to return home, at least for a short time, which hope had been strengthened by the fact that an armistice had been concluded between Germany and France. However, the Princess was

---

* Frederic William.

doomed to disappointment, and the baby boy, whom his father had never yet seen, was christened on the 11th of February, 1871. The Princess writes to her mother as follows on the very day:

"Darmstadt: February 11, 1871.

"To-day our little son is to be christened, but only the family will be present, and my ladies and the two wounded gentlemen, who can get about on crutches now. When I think that the one owes his life to being here, it always gives me pleasure.

"How I shall miss dear Louis to-day! The seven months will be round ere we meet, I fear, and he has never seen his dear little boy. It always makes me sad to look at him, though now I have every reason to hope—please God—that I shall have the joy of seeing Louis come home, and of placing his baby in his arms. My heart is full.

"I will tell Christa* to write an account to you of the christening, for Leopold to see also, as he will be godfather. Frederic William Augustus (after the Empress) Victor (victory) Louis will be his names. Fritz and Vicky, the Empress and Fritz Carl, are godparents."

* Baroness von Schenck, Lady in Waiting to the Princess.

On the 21st of March Prince Louis at last returned home, though only for a short time; but the
beginning of June saw the end of that long and
trying separation. The Prince and Princess went
to Berlin to be present at the entry of the troops on
the 16th of June.

The Prince and Princess spent the autumn with
the Queen at Balmoral. She had not seen her
mother since the war; and she much needed rest
and quiet, somewhat to restore her after all she had
gone through. In November she went to Sandringham, where, soon after her arrival, the Prince of
Wales was taken ill with the same terrible illness
that, ten years before, had proved fatal to the life
of the Prince Consort. The Princess remained with
her sister-in-law during that time, sharing with her
the fearful anxieties of those dark days, and, as
ever, helping when need was greatest. The end of
January 1872 saw her home at Darmstadt, having
left her beloved brother entirely convalescent.

In June of that year a fourth daughter* was

---

* Victoria Alix Helena Louise Beatrice.

born. The year was passed quietly and peacefully. The Princess continued her indefatigable exertions for the welfare of the people at Darmstadt, and more especially turned her attention to bettering the condition of women, and to extending their sphere of employment. The following letter will explain the objects of the great work the Princess had undertaken, and the proceedings of the "Frauentag," or Ladies' Diet, which held its meeting at Darmstadt. At that moment England had sent several delegates to it.

"Darmstadt: October 13.

". . . A few words about our doings here may be of interest to you. The meeting went off well, was very large, the subjects discussed to the purpose and important, and not one word of the emancipated political side of the question was touched upon by anyone. Schools (those of the lower, middle, and higher classes) for girls were the principal theme; the employment of women for post and telegraph offices, &c.; the improvement necessary in the education of nursery maids, and the knowledge of mothers in the treatment of little children; the question of nurses and nursing institutes.

"The public meeting on the following day lasted from nine to two with a small interruption; a committee meeting in the afternoon; and that evening all the members and guests came to us—nearly fifty in number. The following day the meetings lasted even longer, and the English ladies were kind enough to speak—only think, old Miss Carpenter, on all relating to women's work in England (she is our guest here). Her account of the Queen's Institute at Dublin was most interesting. Miss Hill (also our guest), about the boarding-out system for orphans. Miss C. Winkworth, about higher education in England.

"There was a good deal of work to finish afterwards, and a good many members to see. They came from all parts of Germany—many kind-hearted, noble, self-denying women. The presence of the English ladies—above all, of one such as Miss Carpenter, who has done such good work for the reformation of convicts—greatly enhanced the importance of the meeting, and her great experience has been of value to us all. She means still to give a lecture on India and the state of the native schools there, before leaving us."

In November of that year a monument erected to the memory of the Hessian troops who had fallen in the war was unveiled at Metz, the Prince and Princess being present, "besides deputations of officers and men, and the Generals from Metz."*

In the spring of 1873 Princess Alice at last saw one of her fondest daydreams realised—a visit to Italy. She had never really got over the effects of the strain to her health during the time of the great war, and had moreover lately been in much anxiety about little Prince Fritz, so that a complete change was thought essential. Her great love of Art had always made her long to see Rome and Italy, and now that this wish was to be realised she could scarcely believe it. She writes to her mother just before starting:

"Rome is our first halting-place in Italy, and for years it has been my dream and wish to be in that wonderful city, where the glorious monuments of antiquity and of the Middle Ages carry one back to those marvellous times

* Princess Alice's letter to the Queen, November 12, 1872.

"I am learning Italian, and studying the history and art necessary to enable me, in the short time we have, to see and understand the finest and most important monuments. I am so entirely absorbed and interested in these studies just now, that I have not much time for other things."

No journey was ever so enjoyed, or so thoroughly appreciated; but the Princess returned home much fatigued in body, though thoroughly refreshed in mind.

Whilst still in the midst of her joy and thankfulness at being safe home again, and at finding her dear ones "all well and flourishing," a terrible misfortune befell that hitherto so happy home, which for a time seemed to crush the whole brightness out of it. Prince Fritz—the Princess's "darling little Frittie"—was killed by a fall from the window on the 29th of May.

Her husband had left her that very morning on a tour of military inspection. The hour of his departure being so early, the Princess had remained in bed, contrary to her usual habit. The two little Princes came to wish her good morning, and were

left alone with her, as she always tried to accustom
her children from their earliest years to be as independent as possible. The two brothers were
playing at "hide and seek." The Princess's sitting-
room had a large bow window, from which it was
possible to look into one of the bedroom windows.
The Princess always supposed that the little brothers
had wished to look at each other from the opposite
windows; suffice it to say, the elder ran into the
sitting-room, and little Prince Fritz to the bedroom
window as "hard as he could tear," and the impetus
must have shot him out, the windows being half
open and giving way with him. He fell about
twenty feet on to a stone balustrade below. He was
picked up insensible, but outwardly unhurt beyond
a small bruise at the side of his head. The Princess's scream on seeing her child disappear from
her sight has never been forgotten by those who
heard it. Doctors were called hurriedly, and the
first comers were full of hope; but when the Princess's own medical adviser arrived he shook his
head. His familiar acquaintance with the child's
fragile nature made him fear the worst, and in the

evening suffusion of blood on the brain ended that precious little life.

Alone, but calm and collected as ever, the broken-hearted mother had sat all day near that little bed, watching the life so dear to her ebbing slowly away. There was no smile of recognition, but, thank God, there was no struggle and no pain, as the child passed from her care to that of the loving Heavenly Father, who would for ever shield him from all pain and suffering.

Prince Louis, though sent for at once, only reached home after all was over.

The sympathy was universal; and if anything could have brought comfort and solace to the Princess's aching heart, it was the love shown her at that time. Prince Fritz was buried in the mausoleum at the Rosenhöhe, near Darmstadt, on the evening of Whit Sunday, the 1st of June.

The Princess never entirely recovered from this fearful shock—indeed, all her own family felt it had been her "death-blow." A more tender, self-sacrificing mother never lived. All her thoughts

were centred in the welfare of her children; and
though so full of loving care, she was wonderfully
wise in her system of training and education. As
she says herself:

". . . I always think that in the end children
educate the parents. For their sakes there is so
much one must do: one must forget oneself, if
everything is as it ought to be. It is doubly so, if
one has the misfortune to lose a precious child.
Rückert's lovely lines are so true (after the loss of
two of his children):

"Nun hat euch Gott verliehen, was wir euch wollten
              thun,
 Wir wollten euch erziehen, und ihr erzieht uns nun.
 O Kinder, ihr erziehet mit Schmerz die Eltern jetzt;
 Ihr zieht an uns, und ziehet uns auf zu euch zuletzt."*

Though so utterly crushed by the death of her
child, and feeling, like so many that have suffered,

---

* Now unto you the Lord has done what we had wished to do;
  We would have train'd you up, and now 'tis we are train'd
              by you.
  With grief and tears, O children, do you your parents train,
  And lure us on and up to you, to meet in heaven again.

"that one grows to love one's grief as having become part of the thing one loved," still she did not weakly give way to it, but she tried to find a blessing in the hour of trial and grief; she threw herself with energy into her work, and her courage and self-sacrifice were not without a reward; she found indeed, as she so truly said, "the day passes so quickly when one can do good, and make others happy." The visit to England in the autumn did much towards comforting her, and the quiet and rest seemed to restore her to some of her former strength. In the May of the following year, a fifth daughter* was born, and though momentarily disappointed at its not being a boy, this child henceforth became her mother's "sunshine" and comfort.

The years 1875 and 1876 brought outwardly little change in the Princess's life. She continued to take a great interest in politics and in all her favourite schemes; she was able to fulfil her social duties, but her health became gradually but steadily worse. Change of air always seemed to restore her

* Marie Victoria Feodora Leopoldine.

for the time, and she apparently benefited much by visits to England and Scotland, and also to the Black Forest, but the close observer could not fail to see that the improvement was never more than temporary. She herself was fully aware of this, and was often very despondent as to the future. She had over and over again at different times mentioned to one of her sisters* her conviction that she would not live long.

In 1877 the apparent lull in her life was broken by the great strain caused by the illness and death of her father-in-law, whom she dearly loved, followed closely by that of the Grand Duke.

Prince Louis succeeded his uncle as Grand Duke Louis IV. As ever, it fell to the Princess to share the full burden of the trial, and the new life of responsibilities and duties, which came upon her when her physical strength was at a very low ebb, tried her most severely, for with her high sense of duty she could not accept lightly her new position of "Mother of the country" (Landesmutter).

* Princess Christian.

In July of 1878 the Princess came to England
with the Grand Duke and children, and spent some
weeks at Eastbourne. The doctors had insisted on
a thorough change. During her stay there she
endeared herself to high and low. She took the
liveliest interest in all local institutions, helping
where she could, and showing her personal sympathy with the poor by visiting their cottages. Before leaving Eastbourne she made the acquaintance
of Mrs. Vicars, the founder of the Albion Home at
Brighton. She herself paid a visit to that Home,
and afterwards became its patroness. She had at
first refused to do so, not that she did not take the
deepest interest in that good work and long to
help it on, but because she knew the prejudices
existing against such homes. She was deeply im-
pressed by Mrs. Vicars' "wonderful knowledge and
practical power, and by her loving gentle ways
towards those poor girls;" * and this eventually
induced her to take the Home under her protection.
She wrote as follows to Mrs. Vicars:

* Princess Alice's own words.

"New Palace, Darmstadt.

"Dear Mrs. Vicars,

"I have returned from visiting the Home, so convinced of your excellent management of it in every respect, that, if you still feel my becoming Patroness of the Home (and of the Ladies' Association connected with it) can further the good and noble work, I am most willing to comply with your request. The spirit of true, loving, Christian sympathy in which the work was begun by you, and with which it is carried out; the cheerfulness you impart, the motherly solicitude you offer to those struggling to return to a better life, cannot fail to restore in a great measure that feeling of self-respect so necessary to those voluntarily seeking once more a virtuous life, and by so doing regaining the respect of their fellow-creatures. 'Inasmuch as ye have done it unto one of the least of these my brethren, ye have done it unto Me.' In this spirit may the Home, as well as the Association connected with it, continue its good work. My entire sympathy and good wishes will ever be with it.

"Ever yours truly,
"ALICE."

After having settled at home again, the Princess

threw herself with renewed zeal into her work. During her last visit to England she was full of admiration for Miss Octavia Hill, whose acquaintance she had made in England in 1877, and entirely entered into the spirit of her great undertaking, sharing her view "that we must become the friends of the poor to be their benefactors." The Princess was anxious to work on "the same lines" as Miss Hill, and to see similar efforts made in improving the dwellings and condition of the poor at Darmstadt.

Several of the Princess's own family visited her at Darmstadt during the autumn, the very last of them being Prince Leopold. Her happiness at having what she called "a bit of home and of England" with her always seemed to give her fresh strength. But she had scarcely had time to realise how great the happiness of those visits had been before an awful and sudden calamity broke in upon her. On the 8th of November, Princess Victoria was seized with diphtheria; Princess Alix took it next, then little Princess May, after her Princess Irène, then Prince Ernest and the Grand Duke.

The following touching and beautiful account of

those dark days will speak for itself, and will only
deepen the love and admiration already felt for the
beloved Princess. The account is written by a great
personal friend of hers, Miss Macbean, who never
left her during that dreadful time, and whose devotion to her cannot be too much appreciated. Miss
Macbean's family had settled at Darmstadt. The
Princess and the Grand Duke were very intimate
with them, and always considered them amongst
their best and truest friends. Princess Alice's own
lady-in-waiting happened to be away on leave when
the illness broke out, and Miss Macbean was, as
often previously, doing the duty for her.*

"We were having five o'clock tea on Tuesday
afternoon, the 5th of November, 1878, the Grand
Duke and Duchess and myself—they were both in
particularly good spirits—and afterwards we all sat

---

* Miss Macbean left the Princess, to return to England, at
the Princess's express wish, after the Grand Duke and Prince
Ernie were convalescent. The Princess was anxious her dear
friend should have a thorough change and rest after all she had
gone through. This is only another proof of the Princess's unselfish thought for those who were about her.

some time talking, the Princess as usual on her
sofa. She said, 'Katie, you have had the mumps;
isn't it awful pain? I believe Victoria is going to
have them; she has got such a stiff neck, and her
glands seem giving her great pain. Fancy if we
are all ill with the mumps, because I believe it is
very infectious.' Then she called in Princess
Victoria, who was reading to all her sisters and
Prince Ernie in the next room. Princess Victoria
did not hear the call, and I got up and went to
tell her. I saw her sitting on the sofa, with Princesses Ella, Irène, Alix, and May, and Prince Ernie
in a circle close round her, listening intently to a
story she was reading to them. I thought Princess
Victoria looked flushed and not very well; she said
her neck was rather painful, and she couldn't move
her head comfortably about. The subject was then
dropped, as little Princess May was asking her
mother ('Mother dear,' as Her Royal Highness was
teaching her to call her) for some cake and a little
tea, and then she begged me to play, for them all
to dance. Her Royal Highness was reading *Sarche-
don*, and I asked her if it would disturb her, but
she said no, she enjoyed it; so I sat down to the
piano and played every description of thing I could
remember, over and over again, and the children
all danced in the next room for about half an hour.

They were then all sent to bed, Princess Victoria not being allowed to kiss the others on account of the 'mumps.' . . . The next morning Miss Jackson,* Herr v. Dadelsen,** and I were in the schoolroom, when the Princesses came up from breakfast. Princess Victoria came up to me, and we talked for some time, each of us perched on the edge of the table; she kept on whispering to me and telling me 'secrets.' I noticed she looked rather strange, and her neck was so stiff she could not move her head, but she said nothing. The Grand Duchess sent for me, and I ran downstairs. She at once said, 'I can't think what is the matter with Victoria; at breakfast just now it was such pain to her to swallow that it made her cry, and her throat was so painful she ate nothing.' The doctor came that morning, and at once ordered her to be shut up away from the others, and towards luncheon-time we heard it was diphtheria. The Grand Duchess was much alarmed, as Princess Victoria got much worse in the afternoon (that was Wednesday, the 6th of November), and also because, as they had all been at breakfast together, the fear was that she had given it to the other children. Thursday and Friday she

---

* Governess to the young Princesses.
** Tutor to the Hereditary Grand Duke.

continued very ill. Friday the doctor told the dear
Grand Duchess he hoped to pull her through. Then
the illness did not strike one in its horrible strength,
hers being the first case, and the doctor not saying
very much about it to Her Royal Highness. I
hardly left her those days; she had the children a
great deal with her, and I don't think she took in
that the little ones, her pets, could be taken ill. We
went to church as usual on Sunday morning; we
were then all taking desinfectants, and no one was
allowed to come into the palace on account of infection, nor was I allowed to go home.

"The Grand Duchess and I went out driving as
usual on the following Monday, the 11th of November, and that evening we were rather uneasy about
Princess Alix, as she did not appear to be very
well, and on coming down to Her Royal Highness's
room the next morning, she told me that she had
been called up to see her at two o'clock in the
morning, and on looking at her throat had seen
large patches of white membrane; she had at once
sent for the doctor, who declared she had taken it
in a very violent form. Her Royal Highness was
dreadfully anxious, as one of the little ones had
got it, and her great fear was that Princess May
should have the horrible illness. The little one
came into Her Royal Highness's bedroom at about

half-past eight, and rushed up to her mother, clambered on to the bed, and kissed her. I sat on the floor, and we played a long time, close to Her Royal Highness's bed, and she watched us and kept on saying 'My sweet Maysie.' The little one climbed all over me, on my back and shoulders. I thought I had never seen her look so well or in such high spirits, or such a dear sweet little thing as she was that morning romping with me. After breakfast the Princess and I went out, and on going downstairs we saw Princesses Ella, Irène, and May, and Prince Ernest all at the top of the stairs going down also for their drive. Little Princess May smiled and looked so sweet in the little blue hat and ulster she nearly always wore, with her little face covered with dimples and looking the picture of health. At about 12 A.M. Joey* came into Her Royal Highness's sitting-room, and said Princess May did not seem at all well. Her Royal Highness gave me a look that said what she had feared had come; she started up at once and went to the nursery, and there was little Princess May in high fever and spots in her throat. Her Royal Highness was very quiet though deadly anxious, but the little thing was so strong naturally, and in such good health,

---

* Nurserymaid.

that we hoped and almost believed she would be spared. She had it so badly from the first that all our thoughts were given to her. The Princess Alix was very ill. That was Tuesday. On Wednesday morning I was writing a note about half-past nine, when Her Royal Highness came in; she looked *so* ill and worn and wretched, and threw herself down into a chair, and burst into tears, and said, 'Oh, if only my little May is left to me, my little pet, my darling with her precious dimples and loving ways!' She was utterly miserable, but so good and patient. Dr. Eigenbrodt said I ought to go home, but I would not. Her Royal Highness said she was so thankful to have me. Princess Ella and Miss Jackson had been sent the day before to Princess Charles', and Prince Ernie with M. von Dadelsen on the Wednesday. She had ordered the pony carriage at eleven, and then we drove to the Exercirplatz, because she thought the air was so good there. She was so dear and sweet, and said how changed she was in her way of thinking on religion, and how now she was able to bear things much more patiently. All that day Princess May became worse. Every morning the doctor looked at our throats—she said, 'just to be on the safe side. I am quite sure I shall not take the illness.'

"The next morning, Thursday, Princess Irène

was down with the diphtheria; she had been taken ill in the middle of the night, and about ten o'clock the same day Prince Ernie was brought back to the palace, down with the illness too. Princess Victoria was now recovering. After breakfast Her Royal Highness and I drove to her hospital to get a cold-water cushion for Princess May, as her fever was so dreadfully high. Fräulein Helmsdörfer tried to comfort Her Royal Highness in saying that they had had many as bad a case and had cured them, but Her Royal Highness was very anxious; she went often to the door of Princess May's room, but was not allowed in. Princess Ella was quite well, but kept entirely away from the palace. On Thursday evening Her Royal Highness and I went to the service in the English church; special services they were having every day now, and in the other churches the same. They had nearly all her favourite hymns, and when we got home she made me mark them for her in her hymn-book. The last two or three evenings she had sent for Mr. Sillitoe* to read prayers in her room, and she found it such a comfort, she said—she did not think she could have borne it all without them; they were some beautiful prayers for strength for the sick. Friday

* English chaplain at Darmstadt.

was an awful day; all the day the little one continued to get worse, and though very quiet and
calm, the Princess was nearly mad with anxiety and
fear, but even then always thinking of others and
what she could do for them. God gave her wonderful strength to bear it all. All that day we
feared the worst, and Princess May's life, and
Princess Irene's as well, were hanging on a thread.
I had luncheon with the Grand Duke and Duchess,
as I had for the last three days, and he was in a
wild state of what seemed excitement; he was
dreadfully flushed and hot, and said he couldn't
swallow, but kept on whistling and singing all the
time. We thought it looked very bad, but Her
Royal Highness tried to laugh at him, and told him
the port he had been drinking had flushed his face,
and some hazel nuts he had been eating that morning were the cause of his sore throat. However, he
laughed, and said he was going to be ill, teasing
me very much all the time. He sent for a housemaid and had a fire made in the next bedroom
(the Crown Princess's bedroom), and directly after
lunch went and lay down, saying he was going to
sleep. Her Royal Highness said, 'Well, Katie, you
and I are the only ones now left who are not ill,
there is so much to be done and seen after.'

"Whenever she was not going about seeing after

the others, she was lying on her sofa, but too anxious to read or do anything, and I always sat on a chair by her. That evening the little one was almost hopelessly ill, but at about half-past seven she improved a little; she always said, 'If my little one is only left me! What should I do if she were taken away?' I stayed with her till late that night. She looked so sad and worn.

"Next morning, at about five o'clock, Frau Kantner* came to my door and said the Grand Duchess wished me to go down to her room. I went down, and straight up to her bed; she was half sitting up, her face ghastly white; she put out both her arms, and drew me to her, and whispered, 'She is gone; my little darling is dead,' and then burst into tears. And then she told me how it was: that in the middle of the night Dr. Eigenbrodt had come into her room and said there had been an accident, a piece of membrane had crossed the windpipe of the little one, choked her, and in a moment she was gone; that she (the Grand Duchess) had rushed into the nursery, but that it was too late; she sat by the little one a long time, then kissed her and left her, and had spent those hours of misery by herself, and then sent for me. She said,

* Princess's own housemaid.

'It is God's will, but oh that He should have taken that one, my greatest joy and delight in life, my sweet, sweet little May-flower! Do you remember the last time we saw her well, at the top of the stairs before going out driving, and her face covered with those bewitching little dimples?' She continued talking about her for some time, and what she dreaded was having to tell the Grand Duke, which she thought she must do almost directly, as he kept on asking after Princess May. She was very quiet after we had talked about the little one for some time, and made an effort to remain calm; at last she said, 'I must go and tell him; you remain here,' and sat up in bed saying, 'Come and kneel down, and let us ask God for strength for me to tell him and bear it.' Then she got up quite quietly, and went to the Grand Duke's room, where she stayed about a quarter of an hour, after which she came back and got into bed again. She told me that when she had told him, at first he would not believe it, and he then gave a great cry. She said it was heartrending to see his awful grief, and then she herself broke down afresh. She said, 'My little darling! I have said they are not to dress her out, and have told Orchy * only to put on her little

---

* Nurse, who had been with the children since 1866.

6 °

nightgown, and have given one of my lace hand-
kerchiefs for her feet.' She spoke about it quite
quietly, and seemed to make an effort to do so, and
then said, 'She was so especially beloved because
she was the baby and the nearest to me, and used
to kiss and pet me as none of the others do, I suppose because they are older.'

"I don't quite know how we got through that
day. She had Herr von Westerweller, and arranged
all about the funeral. It was a sort of quiet despair,
and she did not seem to comprehend or take it in
that 'the little one' was gone. That whole day, and
for some days after, Prince Ernie's life hung on a
thread; and she used to say, 'Only not him too; if
my boy is taken I shall die too; surely it is enough
to give up *one* child, my best loved little one;' and
she would lie with clasped hands and closed eyes
quite quiet for a long time, till I roused her. Prince
Ernie did not improve, but continued almost getting
worse, and the suspense was dreadful. She was not
able to tell the other children, as they were not
strong enough, and she dreaded so having to tell
them, especially Prince Ernie, as little Princess May
was his special favourite, and they all kept talking
of her and sending her their toys. All Saturday
and Sunday passed, I don't know how; I never left
her except to write letters for her, and she said she

wished to have no one with her but me. The service and funeral was to be that (Monday) afternoon, a short private service taking place in the palace at three o'clock. I asked her in the morning if it would not be a great relief when the day was over, and she said, 'Oh no, why should it be? It will be worse after to-day; it is her last day at home, and to-day they take her away from me altogether.' She was very quiet, almost cheerful, and told me at the service I was to stand directly behind her, and follow after her next into the room. She said two or three times, 'I am so glad it is such a fine bright day for her to go out there (to Rosenhöhe), such bright sunshine, and the birds singing like a spring day—just such a day as she always liked so much.' She spoke very little, and always with her eyes fixed on the sky, and then they would fill with tears; and once she said, 'Fancy having *two* up there in that blue sky, two of my little angels. I wonder if they know that "mother dear" is looking at them, and if my two sweet little loves are looking down at me! Only no more, not Ernie. I could not bear that; it would kill me to have to give him up too.' She then went into her room, putting on the long crape veil that was customary for funerals. Frau Strecker and Fräulein Helmsdörfer were waiting outside in the passage; and just before it was

time to go down to the service she sent the maid
out of her room, and turned round to me, and said,
'It is *so* hard to bear, but let us ask God to give
me strength. My Maysie, my sweet little flower,
they take my heart away with you this afternoon—
away for ever! Never to see her face again, or to
feel her sweet kisses on my face, all blank and
dreary!' Then she was quite calm, and said, 'Now
we must go down; keep close to me all the time,
and if I kneel down be ready to help me up, as I
feel so weak.'

"It was a lovely afternoon, and the sun streamed
in through the glass front door. At the bottom of
the staircase, and in rows facing us as we went
down, stood all the gentlemen of the Court, and
gentlemen filling official posts, and on each side of
the staircase her servants. Past them you saw into
Prince Alfred's room where they had put her 'little
one,' the curtains of the room drawn, and in the
centre the coffin raised and quite buried in masses
of white flowers, on either side large candles burning, and at the head great palm plants. She walked
into the room, her face looking like a mask, and I
kept close to her during the service; on the other
side of the room were all the gentlemen who had
moved in. Just after the clergyman had finished
the service she knelt down close by the coffin and

prayed for a few minutes, then took up a corner of
the white satin pall in her hands and kissed it,
and got up and walked upstairs again; halfway up
she turned round and looked into the hall and
said, 'They are going to take her out of that door,
where she has often gone, but after to-day she will
never come in or go out again.' The carriage (Her
Royal Highness's own) was waiting outside in the
porch, and they were carrying the flowers out as
fast as they could. She then went to the top of
the stairs and told me to watch till they brought
'her' out, and then tell her, which I did, and she
knelt down and looked (and *how* she looked!)
through the banisters, and watched them putting
her into the carriage; and then she and I went into
the Grand Duke's sitting-room, and watched it
all going out of the gates. After that she was
wonderfully quiet, and went and saw the Grand
Duke."

The Princess seemed to feel with renewed keen-
ness the loss of Princess May after Prince Ernest
began to recover. Whilst he was so ill she had to
keep from him the death of his favourite little
sister, and the mere fact of having to do so
seemed to help her over those first sad days;

for her only thought, then as ever, was to try
and help the loved husband and children, whom
she would so gladly have sheltered from all suffering and grief.

On the 6th of December the Grand Duke and
Prince Ernest were sufficiently recovered to go out
in a close carriage, and it was on that day too that
Princess Alice wrote for the last time to her mother.
It was the intention that the whole family should
go in a few days to Heidelberg for change of air.
The Princess herself was most anxious for this
move, and had personally made all the arrangements for it. On the afternoon of the 7th of December, hearing that the Duchess of Edinburgh
would pass through Darmstadt with her children on
her way to England, Princess Alice went to the
station to see her. She had complained all day of
a very bad headache, but did not seem otherwise
more than usually ailing. That evening, however,
the first symptoms of that fatal illness declared
themselves, and the next morning the doctors confirmed the fact of its being diphtheria. The case
was a most severe one from the first, and the Prin-

cess's weakened delicate state made all specially
anxious as to the course it would take.

When first taken ill she had quite given up all
hope of her recovery, and she occupied herself in
writing numerous directions down on slips of paper
for the Grand Duke, also several wishes in case of
her death. As the illness, however, assumed a
more and more hopeless aspect, the Princess herself said she felt better, and also that she was convinced she would "get through it." She suffered
terribly, but through it all her patience, gentleness,
and unselfishness, as ever, made themselves felt;
there never was a thought for herself, only sympathy and consideration for all around.

The Grand Duke was still so weak that he
could not be as constantly with her as he would
have wished, but she was tended with untiring devotion by her nurses, her lady in waiting, and
mother-in-law. On Friday morning, the 13th, the
doctors gave up all hope, and broke it to the poor
husband. All that day she remained perfectly con-
scious, and, as it seemed, unaware of her extreme
danger. She was able to see her mother-in-law

that afternoon, and derived much pleasure from her
visit. Her joy, too, when the Grand Duke entered
her room, was most touching to see, and she bade
him "good night" with her usual bright smile and
with tender words of inquiry after his health. He
knew but too well those were the last words he
would ever hear from her loved lips, and yet, fearful of agitating her or causing her pain, he bade
her "good-night" as if he should meet her on the
morrow. She slept off and on through the day,
and took all the nourishment given her, yet all was
in vain; all the skill and the untiring efforts of the
doctors could not save that precious life. Almost
the last thing she did was to read a letter from her
mother brought her that afternoon by Sir William
Jenner (who had been sent over by the Queen);
she then composed herself to rest, saying, "Now I
will go to sleep again." From that sleep she passed
into unconsciousness, murmuring to herself as a
tired child would do, "From Friday to Saturday—
four weeks—May—dear papa!" Those were her
last words, and early on the morning of the 14th
of December she passed away in her sleep from

the world where she had suffered so much, yet where she had been so happy and so blessed, to that home above where "God shall wipe away all tears from their eyes; and there shall be no more death, neither sorrow nor crying, neither shall there be any more pain, for the former things are passed away."

On the following Tuesday evening, the 17th of December, the loved remains of the Grand Duchess were taken to the chapel in the "Schloss" (Grand-ducal castle), and the next evening to the mausoleum at the Rosenhöhe. (Her two brothers the Prince of Wales and Prince Leopold, as well as her brother-in-law Prince Christian of Schleswig-Holstein, were present.) There she rests between those two children she had "loved so well and lost awhile."

LETTERS.

LETTERS.

———

1862.

Beloved Mama,

Before leaving the yacht I must send you a few lines to wish you once more good-bye, and to thank you again and again for all your kindness to us.

My heart was very full when I took leave of you and all the dear ones at home; I had not the courage to say a word—but your loving heart understands what I felt.

Yesterday, after we reached Bingen, all the Hessian officers of state received us. At every station we received fresh people, and had to speak to them. At Mayence also the beautiful Austrian band played whilst we waited, in pouring rain, which only ceased as we reached Darmstadt. The station before, the Grand Duke, Prince and Princess Charles with their children, Prince Alexander and his wife, received us—all most kind and cordial.

At the station we were again received; the whole town so prettily decked out; the Bürger [Burgesses Escort] rode near our carriage; countless young ladies in white, and all so kind, so loyal: in all the speeches kind and touching allusions were made to you, and to our deep grief. I believe the people never gave so hearty a welcome. We two drove together through the town; incessant cheering and showering of flowers. We got out at Prince and Princess Charles's house, where the whole family was assembled.

We then went to our rooms, which are very small, but so prettily arranged, with such perfect taste, all by my own dear Louis; they look quite English.

We then drove to Bessungen for dinner *en famille.* . . .

We were listening to twelve Sängervereine [Choral Unions] singing together yesterday evening—two hundred people; it was most beautiful, but in pouring rain. Some came upstairs dripping to speak to us. The Grand Duke gave me a fine diamond bracelet he and his wife had ordered for me, and showed me all over his rooms.

To-morrow we receive the Standesherren [Princes and Counts] and the gentlemen of both Houses.

My thoughts, rather *our* thoughts, are constantly with you, beloved Mama. Please give my love to all at home; it is impossible to write to them all.

July 16.

. . . It is extremely hot here. The last two days we rode out at eight in the morning in the wood, where the air is very pleasant, near the ground where the troops are drilled. On Monday we looked on, and the soldiers were so much flattered.

At half-past one on Monday we received the gentlemen of the Upper House, then the Lower House, then the Flügeladjutanten [aides-de-camp], then the Stadtvorstand [Town Council], then about seventy officers, then a deputation of the English here. All these people I had to speak to *en grande toilette*, and at four we drove to a large dinner at the Schloss. The Grand Duke led me, and I always sit near him.

Yesterday at three the whole family drove to Seeheim, a lovely place in the mountains, to dinner with the Grand Duke. In the two villages we

passed, flowers were showered upon us, and the
Pfarrer [clergyman] made a speech.

I am really deeply touched by the kindness and
enthusiasm shown by the people, which is said to
be quite unusual. They wait near the house to see
us, and cheer constantly—even the soldiers.

We then drove for tea, which is always at eight,
to Jugenheim to Prince Alexander, whose birthday
it was, and did not get home till ten.

The whole family are very amiable towards me,
and Prince Alexander is most clever and amusing.

Darling Louis is very grateful for your kind
messages. We talk and think of you often, and
then my heart grows very heavy. Away from home
I cannot believe that beloved Papa is not there; all
is so associated with him.

July 19.

Beloved Mama,

Many thanks for your last kind letter, and all
the news from home; dear Baby [Princess Beatrice]
is the only one you have mentioned nothing of, and
I think of her so often.

Some people are coming to us at one, and then
the whole Ministerium [Administration]. It is really
so difficult to find something to say to all these
people, and they stand there waiting to be spoken to.

Yesterday we received a deputation from Giessen, with a very pretty dressing-case they brought us as a present.

On Thursday we went incognito with Prince Alexander and his wife to Frankfurt. The town is decked out most beautifully, and countless Schützen [riflemen] are walking about in their dress. We dined at the Palais and then sat in the balcony.

I have just taken leave of dear Lady Churchill and General Seymour.* They have made themselves most popular here, and the people have been very civil to them.

Louis and I have begun reading *Westward Ho!* together.

The Grand Duke went all the way to Kranichstein for me the other day, and walked about till he was quite hot. He has forbidden my visiting the other places until his return, as he wishes to lead me about there himself. I do not see very much of the other relations save at meals; and, having our own carriages, we two drive together mostly alone. We have tea usually out of doors in some pretty spot we drive to.

These lines will find you in Windsor. I went

* Afterwards Marquis of Hertford, who died on the 25th of January, 1884.

out this morning and tried to find some of those
pretty wreaths to send you, but could get none.
Please put one in St. George's* from me. It is the
first time you go to that hallowed spot without me;
but in thought and prayer I am with you. May
God strengthen and soothe you, beloved Mama, and
may you still live to find some ray of sunshine on
your solitary path, caused by the love and virtue of
his children, trying, however faintly, to follow his
glorious example!

I do strive earnestly and cheerfully to do my
duty in my new life, and to do all that is right,
which is but doing what dear Papa would have
wished.

July 20.

Thousand thanks for your dear long letter of the
18th just received. How well do I understand your
feelings! I was so sad myself yesterday, and had
such intense longing after a look, a word from beloved Papa! I could bear it no longer. Yet *how*
much worse is it not for you! You know, though,
dear Mama, *he* is watching over you, waiting for
you. The thought of the future is the one sustain-

---

* St. George's Chapel, Windsor, where the Prince Consort
rested until removed to the Mausoleum at Frogmore.

ing, encouraging point for all. "They who sow in tears shall reap in joy;" and great joy will be yours hereafter, dear Mama, if you continue following that bright example. . . .

We usually get up about a quarter or half-past seven, and take some coffee at eight. Then we either go out till ten or remain at home, and till twelve I write and arrange what I have to do.

At one, when we return from breakfast, we usually read together. I have still a. great many people to see, and they usually come at two.

At four is dinner, and at half-past five we are usually back here, and occupy ourselves till six or seven, then drive out somewhere for tea at eight, walk about, and return at a quarter or half-past ten. We do not waste our time, I assure you, and Louis has a good deal to do at this moment.

Mr. Theed's bust of dear Papa must be very lovely. I am curious to hear what you think of Marochetti's.* It will be very sad for you to see.

A fortnight already I am here, and away from my dear home three weeks! How much I shall have to tell you when we meet. My own dear Mama, I do love you so much! You know, though

---

* The recumbent statue of the Prince Consort, now in the Mausoleum at Frogmore.

silent, my love and devotion to you is deep and
true.   If I could relinquish part of my present happiness to restore to you some of yours, with a full
heart would I do it; but God's will be done!   God
sustain my precious mother! is the hourly prayer of
her loving and sympathising child.

July 24.

. . . You tell me to speak to you of *my* happiness—our happiness.   You will understand the
feeling which made me silent towards you, my own
dear bereaved Mother, on that point; but you are
unselfish and loving and can enter into my happiness, though I could never have been the first to
tell you how intense it is, when it must draw the
painful contrast between your past and present
existence.   If I say I love my dear husband, that
is scarcely enough—it is a love and esteem which
increases daily, hourly; which he also shows to me
by such consideration, such tender loving ways.
What was life before to what it has become now?
There is such blessed peace being at his side, being
his wife; there is such a feeling of security; and
we two have a world of our own when we are together, which *nothing* can touch or intrude upon.
My lot is indeed a blessed one; and yet what have
I done to deserve that warm, ardent love which my

darling Louis ever shows me? I admire his good
and noble heart more than I can say. How he
loves you, you know, and he will be a good son to
you. He reads to me every day out of *Westward
Ho!* which I think very beautiful and interesting.

This morning I breakfasted alone, as he went
out with his regiment. I always feel quite impatient until I hear his step coming upstairs, and
see his dear face when he returns.

Yesterday, and the previous night, I thought of
you constantly, and of our last journey together to
dear Balmoral. Sad, painful though it was, I liked
so much being with you, trying to bear some of
your load of sorrow with you. From here I share
all as if I were really by your side; and I think so
many fervent prayers cannot be offered to a merci-
ful loving God without His sending alleviation and
comfort.

Please remember me to Grant, Brown, and all
of them at home in dear Scotland, and tell them
how much I wish, and Louis also, that we were
there, changed though everything is.

Darmstadt: August 1.

. . . My heart feels ready to burst when I think
of such sorrow as yours. I pray my adored Louis

may long be spared to me. If you only knew how dear, how loving he is to me, and how he watches over me, dear darling!

To-morrow we go to Coburg, which was an old promise. Dear Uncle* sent only two days ago to say he left Coburg on the 5th, and would we not come before? You will understand that, happy beyond measure as I am to go there, a lump always comes into my throat when I think of it—going for the first time with Louis to dear Papa's house, where but recently he showed us everything himself.** Dear Mama, I think I can scarcely bear it —the thought seems so hard and cruel. He told us as children so much of Coburg, spoke to us of it with such childlike affection, enjoyed so much telling us every anecdote connected with each spot; and now these silent spots seem to plead for his absence.

To see the old Baron [Stockmar] will be a great happiness, and that Louis should make his acquaintance.

Calenberg bei Coburg: August 4.

Once more in dear Coburg, and you can fancy

---

* Duke of Saxe-Coburg Gotha.
** This was in the autumn of 1860.

with what feelings. Everything reminds me of beloved Papa and of our last happy visit.

We are living here, and yesterday we spent all the afternoon and dined at the Rosenau. It was a lovely day, and the view so beautiful. We went all over the house and walked about in the grounds. We walked to dear Papa's little garden, and I picked two flowers there for you, which I enclose.

Every spot brought up the remembrance of something dear Papa had told us of his childhood; it made me so sad, I can't tell you. Uncle Ernest was also sad, but so kind and affectionate, and they both seemed so pleased at our having come.

Everything about dear Papa's illness, and then of the sad end, I had to tell. I lived the whole dreadful time over again, and wonder, whilst I speak of it, that we ever lived through it.

At nine o'clock Church service was in the pretty little chapel. Holzei read, and Superintendent Meyer preached a most beautiful sermon, the text being where our Saviour told His disciples they must become as a little child to enter into the kingdom of heaven. He spoke with his usual fervour, and it was most impressive. I saw him afterwards, and he inquired very much after you.

We are going after breakfast to the Festung,

and then Louis and I are going to see the dear Baron [Stockmar].

August 9.

Next Monday we are going to Auerbach, to live there for a little time. It lies in the Bergstrasse, and is very healthy. The Grand Duke allows us to inhabit one of the houses.

August 16.

. . . How I long to read what Mr. Helps has written about Papa! What can it be but beautiful and elevating, if he has rightly entered into the spirit of that pure and noble being?*

Oh, Mama! the longing I sometimes have for dear Papa surpasses all bounds. In thought he is ever present and near me; still we are but mortals, and as such at times long for him also. Dear good Papa! Take courage, dear Mama, and feel strong in the thought that you require all your moral and physical strength to continue the journey which brings you daily nearer to *Home* and to *Him!* I know how weary you feel, how you long to rest

---

* This refers to Mr., afterwards Sir, Arthur Helps's Introduction to the *Collected Addresses and Speeches of the Prince Consort*, which was then about to be published (Murray, 1862).

your head on his dear shoulder, to have him to soothe your aching heart. You will find this rest again, and how blessed will it not be! Bear patiently and courageously your heavy burden, and it will lighten imperceptibly as you near him, and God's love and mercy will support you. Oh could my feeble words bring you the least comfort! They come from a trusting, true and loving heart, if from naught else.

Auerbach: August 16.

. . . We do feel for you so deeply, and would wish so much to help you, but there is but One who can do that, and you know whom to seek. He will give you strength to live on till the bright day of reunion. . . .

Auerbach: August 21.

. . . Our visit to Giessen * went off very well. The people were most loyal. We went to see the Gymnasts, and Louis walked about amongst them, which pleased them very much. He is very popular there, and I am very glad we both went, for it made a good impression.

We drove to Louis' property, Stauffenberg, a

---

* During a Musical and Gymnastic Festival.

beautiful (alas! ruined) castle, which by degrees he is having restored, and which will be a charming house for us, if it is finished, which can only be done gradually.

Auerbach: August 23.

. . . Try and gather in the few bright things you have remaining and cherish them, for, though faint, yet they are types of that infinite joy still to come. I am sure, dear Mama, the more you try to appreciate and to find the good in that which God in His love has *left* you, the more worthy you will daily become of that which is in store. That earthly happiness you had is indeed gone for ever, but you must not think that every ray of it has left you. You have the privilege, which dear Papa knew so well how to value, in your exalted position, of doing good and living for others, of carrying on his plans, his wishes into fulfilment, and as you go on doing your duty, this will, this must, I feel sure, bring you peace and comfort. Forgive me, darling Mama, if I speak so openly; but my love for you is such that I cannot be silent, when I long so fervently to give you some slight comfort and hope in your present life.

I have known and watched your deep sorrow with a sympathising, though aching heart. Do not think that absence from you can still that pain. My love for you is strong, is constant; I would like to shelter you in my arms, to protect you from all future anxiety, to still your aching longing! My own sweet Mama, you know I would give my life for you, could I alter what you have to bear!

Trust in God! ever and constantly. In *my* life I feel that to be my stay and my strength, and the feeling increases as the days go on. My thoughts of the future are bright, and this always helps to make the minor worries and sorrows of the present dissolve before the warm rays of that light which is our guide.

Auerbach: August 25.

. . . To-day is the Ludwigstag, a day kept throughout the country, and on which every Ludwig receives presents, &c.; but we spend it quite quietly. Louis' parents and the others are coming to breakfast, and remain during the day. Louis is out riding. We always get up early. He rides whilst I write, and we then walk together and breakfast somewhere out of doors.

We went to the little church here yesterday, which is very old, and they sang so well.

I drew out of doors also, as it was very fine; but it is very difficult, as it is all green, and the trees are my misfortune, as I draw them so badly. I play sometimes with Christa;* she plays very well.

August 26 [Prince Consort's Birthday].

With a heavy heart do I take up my pen to write to you to-day—this dear day, now so sad, save through its bright recollections. I cannot bear to think of it now, with no one to bring our wishes to, with that painful silence where such mirth and gaiety used to be. It is very hard to bear, and the first anniversary is like the commencement of a new epoch in our deep sorrow.

When your dear present was brought to me this morning, I could not take my eyes from it, though they were blinded with tears. Oh, those beautiful, those loved features! There wants but his kind look and word to make the picture alive! Thousand thanks for it, dear Mama.

How trying this day will be for you! My thoughts are constantly with you, and I envy the privilege the others have in being near you and being able to do the least thing for you.

The sun shines brightly in the still blue sky;

---

* The Princess's lady, Baroness Christa Schenck.

how bright and peaceful it must be where our dear
Spirit dwells, if it is already so beautiful here.

September 5.

. . . Two days ago, Louis and I went to Worms.
Whilst he went to his regiment, which the Grand
Duke came to inspect, I went to the Dom, which
is most beautiful; and then went in a little boat
on the Rhine, which was charming. It took us,
driving, an hour and a half from Auerbach to
Worms.

Auerbach: September 7.

. . . For Louis' birthday we are going to Darmstadt; it is getting cold and damp here, and the
house is small. We take our meals in another
house, and it is cold to walk over there of an
evening. Think of us on the 12th. It was such a
happy day last year.*

I have such *Heimweh* [yearning] after beloved
Papa; it is dreadful sometimes when I think of him
and of our home. But he is so happy in his bright
home, could we but catch a glimpse of him there.
Dear Grandmama [the Duchess of Kent], too, is

* Prince Louis was then at Balmoral.

constantly in my thoughts lately. I can see her
before me—so dear, kind, and merry. As time goes
on, such things only mingle themselves more vividly
with one's usual life; for it is their *life* which is
nearest us again, and not their *death*, which casts
such a gloom over their remembrance.

Auerbach: September 11.

. . . How beautiful Heidelberg is! we went all
over the Castle, and with such glorious weather.
There is one side still standing, built and decorated
by a pupil of Michael Angelo, which dear Papa
admired so much. How do I miss not being able
to talk to beloved Papa of all I see, hear, feel,
and think! His absence makes such a gap in my
existence.

Darmstadt: October 13.

. . . Our visit to Baden was charming, and dear
Fritz and Louise* so kind! Louis and I were both
delighted by our visit. The Queen, the Duchess of
Hamilton, and Grand Duchess Hélène were there,
besides dear Aunt [Princess Hohenlohe], and Countess Blücher. The two latter dear and precious as
ever.

* Grand Duke and Grand Duchess of Baden.

We left yesterday morning; spent three hours
with Grand Duchess Sophie,* who is the most
agreeable, clever, amiable person one can imagine.
It gave me real pleasure to make her acquaintance.
Aunt Feodore's house, though small, is really very
pretty, and her rooms are hung full of pictures. I
saw Winterhalter also, in his lovely new house,
which he has gone and sold, saying it was too
good for him. He has painted a most beautiful
picture of the Grand Duchess Hélène — quite
speaking.

. . . I am going to make my will before leaving.
I do not like leaving (for England) without having
done something.

Darmstadt: October 17.

First of all, thousand thanks from Louis and me
for your having allowed dear Arthur** to come to
us. I cannot tell you what pleasure it has been to
me to have that dear child a little bit. He has
won all hearts, and I am so proud when they admire my little brother, who is a mixture of you and
adored Papa.

---

* Grand Duchess of Baden, mother of the reigning Grand
Duke.

** Duke of Connaught, then twelve years old.

Darmstadt: October 23.

. . . We intend probably leaving this on Saturday, the 8th, remaining until the 10th at Coblenz, from whence we go direct in eleven hours and three-quarters to Antwerp, leaving Antwerp the morning of the 12th, to reach Windsor that evening or the next morning.

We always continue reading together, and have read *Hypatia*, a most beautiful, most interesting, and very learned and clever book, which requires great attention.

I have the great bore to read the newspapers every day, which I must do; see Dr. Becker* from eleven to twelve; then I write, and have constantly people to see, so that I have scarcely any time to draw or to play. I also read serious books to myself.

Louis would like to go to Leeds and Manchester from Osborne, as he wants to go to London from Windsor. I shall accompany him sometimes.

October 25.

As you come later to Windsor, we shall not leave till the 10th, remain the 11th with the Queen, then

---

* The Princess Alice's private secretary.

go direct to Antwerp. If the weather is bad we shall wait. Then on the 14th or 15th we shall be at Windsor, which we prefer to coming to Osborne. We hope this will suit you.

All are full of lamentations at our departure, and for so long, which is most natural; but they are very kind. We have a family dinner in our little room to-day, which is large enough for a few people. The Grand Duke has quite lost his heart to Arthur, and Bertie [Prince of Wales] pleased him also very much.

In talking together last night, Louis said what I feel so often, that he always felt as if it must come right again some time, and we should find dear Papa home again. In another *home* we shall.

October 30.

The Grand Duke was quite overcome when I gave him the photographs, and with Baby's [Princess Beatrice's] he is quite enchanted, and wishes me to tell you how grateful he is, and how much he thanks you. You cannot think *how* pleased he was, and the more so that *you* sent them him. He has a warm heart and feels very much for you, and takes warm interest in all my brothers and sisters.

I am glad you are going to see dear Fritz of

8 *

Baden; he will be so pleased. We shall see Louise at Coblenz.

The plans for our house are come, and even the simplest is far above what we poor mortals can build.

November 6.

. . . Yesterday, Mrs. Combe, widow of George Combe and daughter of Mrs. Siddons, came to see me, and was some time with me. Such a clever, amiable old lady. It gave me such pleasure to see and talk with her. Will you tell Sir James Clark so, as she is an old friend of his?

1863.

Marlborough House: May 14.

Dearest Mama,

Our parting this morning was most painful to both of us—from you to whom we *owe* so much, and whom we love so dearly.

May God comfort and support you, beloved Mama, on your sad and weary pilgrimage!

Marlborough House: May 16.

I could not get your dear face and your sweet voice out of my mind for an instant, and everywhere I thought I must see you or dear Papa. It seemed so strange; I had the tears in my eyes all day. The worst was the Opera, for I had never been without you or Papa, and all was the same and yet so different! It was very trying to me; and so will the Drawing-room be to-day. . . . I saw Lady Jocelyn, Duchess of Manchester, Sir Charles Locock, and Lord Alfred Paget, to show them Baby, and all find

her like what we all were. How much *we* have to
thank for in her name. Your affection for her and
all you have done for her have touched us more
than I can say. It seemed to me quite wrong to
take her from you.

On Wednesday, Alix [Princess of Wales] and
myself go to the studios. This morning we drove
in Battersea Park.

May 19.

. . . The Drawing-room was long, but Alix and
I were not so tired, considering the length of time,
for we stood, excepting twenty minutes, in the
middle, when there was a block and the people
could not come.

In to-day's letter you mention again your wish
that we should soon be with you again. Out of the
ten months of our married life five have been spent
under your roof, so you see how ready we are to be
with you. Before next year Louis does not think
we shall be able to come; at any rate when we can
we shall, and I hope we shall be able to see you
for a day or two in Germany to divide the time.

Darmstadt: May 23.

. . . Baby* has been so much admired, and all
the clothes you gave her.

<hr>

* Princess Victoria of Hesse.

Darmstadt: May.

I shan't have time to write more than a few words, as we have just returned from church, and are going to Mayence till Wednesday. The Grand Duke came all the way to Kranichstein yesterday to go about with us, and see how to arrange it comfortably. He is most kind, and sat an hour with me.

We have received two deputations this morning, and my things, which ought to have been here before us, only arrived to-day.

Mayence: June 2.

Now when I return I shall have to unpack and pack again for Kranichstein, and arrange the house there, which has not been lived in for eighty years, so that for writing I have barely a moment.

I have good accounts of Baby, whom all the old gentlemen run out of their houses to look at when she walks in the garden, and try to tell Moffat [her nurse] what they think of her, but she of course understands nothing.

Darmstadt: June 3.

I write to you to-day, as Louis is going for all day to Worms to-morrow, and I am going to Jugenheim to Uncle Alexander. It is already warm here, and we are going in a day or two into the country.

The Queen of Prussia passes through here to-day, and I shall probably hear from her what her intentions are about England. I have received a splendid bracelet from the Empress of Russia—for Baby's picture. She is said to be far from well.

Darmstadt: June 6.

. . . Louis was away from four o'clock yesterday morning till eleven at night. He was at Worms with Uncle Louis. Tuesday is his birthday, and we shall very likely go on Monday to Mayence, as Uncle Louis is always wishing for us.

I took a walk at Jugenheim yesterday with Uncle Alexander,* his wife and children, of more than two hours, and it was so beautiful, and numberless little birds singing. Uncle Alexander was so grateful for all your kindness, and was above all so charmed with you. It always makes me so happy to be able to talk about you, and to hear you appreciated as you ought to be, darling Mama.

June 8.

. . . Baby sits up quite strong, and looks about

* Prince Alexander of Hesse, uncle of Prince Louis of Hesse.

and laughs. She has got on wonderfully, and she
is so good. She was an hour with us yesterday
evening wide awake, and so good. She is as well
and as strong as any child could be. To-day we
go to Mainz, and to-morrow night from thence to
Kranichstein. All our beds must be moved mean-
while, as there are none in the house.

Kranichstein: June 12.

Louis went at six this morning to Darmstadt for
the inspection of his regiment by Uncle Louis.
Princess Charles's birthday is on the 18th. The
Grand Duke will be at Friedberg, and we are to go
for the day, which will be rather tiring, as it is a
good way by rail and back again, and we have to
wait an hour at Frankfort.

Louis is going to take his seat in the Chamber
on the 23rd. He was unable to do so last year, as
we left for England two days before the time.

June 19.

. . . You ask me again if I occupy myself much
and seriously? Not a moment of the day is wasted,
and I have enough to read and to think about:
what with the many and different papers, and inter-

esting books. Dr. Becker comes daily, and I have
a good deal to look after.

June 23.

. . . You will be amused to hear that I have
taken a little black (a Malay) into my service. He
is a dear good boy, was brought over two years
ago by a gentleman, to whom he was given away
by his own parents as a mark of gratitude for some
service done. This man has had him here two
years, but has never had him taught anything. He
has no religion, and can neither read nor write. I
am going to have him taught, and, later, christened.
He is very intelligent, thirteen years old.

We shall remain here for the present; we go
about a good deal seeing things near by, and then
it is the first time we have our household and stable,
so that on account of Haushaltung [housekeeping],
&c., we are going to remain here for a little time.
It is very pleasant besides, and constant moving is
far too expensive for us. We give dinners here,
which are also useful, as I know so few people.
Some of the Standesherren are coming to-morrow,
and later some of the Abgeordneten [Deputies] of
the Second Chamber, which will give us an opportunity of making the acquaintance of some of
the Liberals in the country.

I cannot get rid of my rheumatism, which is so unpleasant.

Louis is very busy; he reads to me sometimes out of Lord Macaulay's last volume of the English History, which I had not yet read. Twice a week Louis takes drill with his cavalry regiment, and he has to ride out at six in the morning, as it is some way off.

June 27.

. . . I bathe every morning and swim about; there is a nice little bathing-house.

I hear Baby shrieking out of doors; she does not cry very much, but she is very passionate. She was vaccinated two days ago by Dr. Weber, and I am going to be done next week; the small-pox is at Darmstadt, and a man died of it yesterday. Louis is very industrious and busy; he has all the papers of the Stände [State papers] to read and look through, and reads other useful books, besides papers and other things which he must read. He wrote to Lord Derby to express his thanks for having been made a Doctor at Oxford. He takes a great deal of exercise, riding, walking, rowing, swimming. We get up at six every morning, and go to bed after ten.

Louis has always a good deal to do at home,

and a good many things which would never be expected of him in England. He knows the necessity and importance of working. I hope next month Uncle Ernest* will come to us for a day on his way back from Homburg. He has asked us for a few days to the Calenberg whilst you are in Germany, and then in the winter we hope to be for a few days at Gotha.

The Lützows,** and Miss Seymour dine with us to-day.

June 30.

To-morrow is our dear wedding-day. With what gratitude do I look back to that commencement of such happiness, and such real and true love, which even daily increases in my beloved husband. Oh! may we not be deprived of it too soon! I admire and respect him for his true-hearted, generous, unselfish, and just nature! Oh, dear Mama, if you only knew how excellent he is! I wish I were good like him, for he is free from any selfish, small or uncharitable feelings. You should see how he is beloved by all his people; our servants adore him.

---

* Duke of Saxe-Coburg-Gotha.
** Count Lützow was at this time the Austrian Minister and Plenipotentiary at the Court of Darmstadt.

I open my heart to you, who have so warm and sympathising a heart, that even in the midst of such deep grief and sorrow as yours will listen to what your children, who love you so dearly, long to say.

Our little one is grown so pretty; she has little pink cheeks, and is so fat and so good-humoured. I often think her like you when she smiles.

July 2.

You can fancy how much we thought of this day last year, and of you and all the love and kindness you showed us then. How truly we both love you, and, when we can, how willingly we shall come to your side, and be of the least use to you, you know, for I feel for you and with you, more than words can describe.

Our first large dinner yesterday went off very well. We make our arrangements, sitting, &c., all as you and dear Papa had it, which is new here, but, I am happy to say, approved of. We always dine at four. Baby appeared afterwards, and really never cries when she is shown, but smiles, and seems quite amused. She is immensely admired, particularly for her healthy appearance and fine large eyes. I really think her like you now; she is

very much changed, and, when she sits up, looks so
pretty and dear.

July 4.

Shortly we are going to pay Prince Solms-Lich,
the President of the First Chamber, a visit. He is
very liberal on the whole, rich, and a nice old
gentleman. He knew Grandpapa in the year 1820,
also Uncle Charles, Uncle Hohenlohe, Aunt Feodore,
and Eliza.* Lady Fife, Annie,** and Mr. Corbett
from Frankfort are coming to us to-day.

The Grand Duke of Weimar was here yesterday
for dinner at the Schloss.

What you say about Germany is so true; and
Louis has the real good of his country near at heart.
They always have to vote for or against what the
Second Chamber brings forward, and the other day
a vote was sent in from the Liberals for an altera-
tion of a Press Law. Only one voice in the whole
Chamber was for it, which was Louis', and this produced a very good effect among the Liberals. He
is no coward, and will say what he thinks, if it is
necessary, even if all are against him.

---

* Princess Hohenlohe's eldest daughter, who died at
Venice.

** Lady Fife's eldest daughter, now Marchioness of Towns-
end.

Kranichstein: July 15.

To-day is Uncle Alexander's birthday, and we have to drive for dinner to Seeheim. To-morrow morning we leave for Lich at five in the morning.

Two nights ago a horrid and *schauerliches* [appalling] event took place here. I went out about eight down to the pond, which is close to the house, to meet Louis. I met an odd-looking pale man, who neither bowed nor looked about, walking slowly along; and when I joined Louis he asked me if I had seen him, as he had been prowling about all the afternoon. We stopped a little longer, when at the end our grooms were running. We rowed on to see what was the matter, and on coming near, a body was floating in the water, the face already quite blue and lifeless. I recognised him at once. Louis and the others with trouble fished him out and laid him in our boat to bring him on shore. It was very horrid to see. We brought him on shore, tried all means to restore him to life, but of no avail. He was carried into the stable. He had committed suicide, and we heard afterwards that he was a very bad character. You can fancy that it was very unpleasant to me, to have that disfigured corpse next me in the boat: and it haunts me now—for a violent death leaves frightful traces, so unlike anything else. But half or quarter of an

hour before, I had passed that man in life, and so
shortly after to see him floating by quite lifeless! It
brings death before one in its worst form, when one
sees a *bad man* die by his own hand. The indif-
ference with which the other people treated it, and
dragged him along, was also revolting to one's feelings; but one must be manly, and not mind those
things; yet I own it made me rather sick, and prevented my sleep that night.

I am glad we are going away for a few days;
the change will be pleasant.

It was such a pleasure to me to have seen dear
Lady Frances Baillie the other day, and she was
looking well, though she is very thin.

You kindly gave me our dear Papa's Farm Book
for the Farmers' Union here; the people are so
touched and pleased. I send you the letter of thanks
to read.

Lich: July 18.

. . . We leave to-morrow afternoon for Frankfort,
and the next day we go to Homburg on the way
home. The Prince and Princess are most kind and
civil; they have a fine Schloss, and are rich. The
latter is clever and amiable, and the young people
—their nephews and nieces—are very nice and
very kind. It is a fine rich country, and they seem

very much beloved. The sister of the Princess, Princess Solms-Laubach, *née* Büdingen, is here also. Her husband was in the Prussian service, and they lived at Bonn whilst dear Papa was there. He came to see them and to spend the evening there very often. She told me how handsome he then was, and how much praised and liked by all. She asked after Rath Florschütz,* after Eos,** and if dear Papa continued later on to be so sleepy of an evening, as he was even then.

Kranichstein: July 21.

Our visit at Lich went off very well. Everything is so "vornehm" [in such good style] and so well arranged.

July 23.

We are going to give Heinrich*** a rendezvous somewhere, perhaps at Kreuznach, which is not very far. On August 1 we are going to the north of the country—a part which I do not know—and on the way we stop at Giessen, where we have been in-

---

* Tutor of the Prince Consort during his boyhood and early youth.

** A favourite greyhound of the Prince Consort's, which he brought to England at the time of his marriage.

*** Prince Henry of Hesse, brother of Prince Louis.

vited to see an Agricultural Exhibition. On Monday we give a tea and a dance—between fifty and sixty people. The advantage of this place is its nearness to Darmstadt, and that there is room enough to receive people.

The Russian and French ambassadors, with their wives, and Mr. Corbett and Lord Robert S. Kerr, dine with us to-day.

July 27.

I have no news to give. To-night we give our first large party—seventy people.

August 1.

Yesterday we were all day at Rumpenheim: so kindly received! The Landgrave, his two brothers Frederic and George, the Dowager Duchess of Mecklenburg-Strelitz, her daughter Duchess Caroline, Aunt Cambridge, Mary,* Augusta** and Adolphus;*** Fritz† and Anna of Hesse and good Princess Louise,†† kindness itself. Aunt Cambridge

---

  * Princess Mary of Cambridge.

 ** Grand Duchess of Mecklenburg-Strelitz.

*** Hereditary Grand Duke of Mecklenburg-Strelitz.

  † Landgrave and Landgravin of Hesse.

 †† Princess Louise of Hesse, sister of the Duchess of Cambridge.

was very amiable, and spoke most tenderly of you.
To-morrow morning Louis goes to Oberhessen, where
I join him in two days. I go to see Uncle Alexander
at Jugenheim; go on Monday to Friedberg, where
there is an asylum for blind people, of which I am
Protectorin [Patroness]. I go to see it, and sleep
at the Castle. The next day I stop on my road to
see Marburg, and shall be in the evening at Als-
feld, where I find Louis. The next day I go on to
Herr von Riedesel at Altenburg, where I breakfast,
and I dine and spend the night with another
Riedesel family at Eisenbach. Louis joins me that
evening. The next day we go on through the
country, as the people are anxious to see us, and
the country is very beautiful. On Thursday and
Friday we shall be at Giessen, on Saturday at
home.

Giessen: August 7.

I am very hot and tired; we have only just
reached this place, and have to go out almost immediately to see the animals and machines.

Our journey has been most prosperous, but
rather tiring, and the heat quite fearful. We were
most kindly received everywhere. English, Hessian,
German flags everywhere, and "Gesangvereine" of
an evening.

9 *

Last night we slept at Schotten, and posted from thence to-day through a lovely, rich, wooded and mountainous district, the Vogelsberg.

We have had but one room everywhere, and have remained only long enough at a place to see it, so that writing has been impossible. To-morrow evening we return to Kranichstein, and then I will write to you an account of everything. Here, with no time, and such heat and noise, it is impossible.

Kranichstein: August 9.

. . . We went, when I last wrote to you at Giessen, to see the different machines at work, in a crowd close round us and a smothering heat. It was interesting, though, in spite of all. The people cheered and were very civil. That day, at the meeting of the agriculturists, Count Laubach told me dear Papa's book lay on the table, and is of the greatest use and interest. I am so pleased to have been the first in Germany to make known something of Papa's knowledge in this science, one of the many in which dear Papa excelled. The people are so grateful to you for having sent it. In the evening the president and some other scientific gentlemen came to tea with us. I was so glad to see how pleased the people were at the interest

Louis takes in these things. A procession was really very pretty; large carts, decorated with the different agricultural emblems, peasants in their different costumes—it was something quite new to me.

At Marburg, I saw in the beautiful church the grave of St. Elizabeth, the castle where she lived, and many other things which Kingsley mentions in his *Saint's Tragedy.*

This week the Emperor of Austria and other potentates came to Frankfort. The King of Prussia has refused, so that now, as it is not a universal meeting, it will not be what it might have been.

Buckingham Palace: October 28.

Thousand thanks for your dear lines! How sad that we should be reduced to writing again! It was such a happiness to speak to you, and in return to hear all you had to say—to try and soothe you, and try to make your burthen lighter. I always feel separation from you so much, for I feel for and with you, more, oh, far more, than I can ever express! I can only say again, trust, hope, and be courageous, and every day will bring something in the fulfilment of all your great duties—which will bring you peace, and make you feel that you are not forsaken, that God has heard your prayer, felt for you, as a loving

Father would, and that dear Papa is not far from you.

Darmstadt: November 2.

Before going out (half-past six) I begin these lines. You will have heard what an awful passage we had. Christa and I had one of those cabins near the paddle-box, and good old May* was with us. Each wave that broke on the ship Christa and I groaned, and May exclaimed, "Oh, goodness, gracious me! what an awful sea! Lord bless you, child, I hope it is all safe!" and so on. If we had not been so wretched, and had not looked so awful with those mountains of waves about us, I should have laughed. All the maids and Moffat were sick. Baby was sick all over her nice new shawl, which was a great grief.

Uncle Louis and Uncle Gustav** received us at the station. My parents-in-law don't return till Wednesday. Yesterday Uncle Louis gave us a large dinner, and to-day he dines *en famille* in our house with Prince Adalbert of Bavaria, Uncle Gustav, and ourselves.

---

* Mrs. Hull, a former nurse of the Princess and her brothers and sisters.

** Prince Gustav Wasa, first cousin to Prince Charles of Hesse.

I was quite done up by this journey. At four in the morning we changed carriages at Cologne, and did not get here .till past twelve o'clock—twenty-nine hours under way.

November 5.

. . . Yesterday evening Louis and I were at a chemical lecture, which was very interesting, by young Hallwachs, the brother of the one Becker spoke to you about.

Our house is getting on very well, and we are often there.

Louis is very grateful and touched by your kind message, and kisses your hand. He is often away for those tiresome Jagden [shooting-parties] from five in the morning till eight at night, as it is some way off.

November 14.

It is not yet eight, and I have such cold fingers. The messenger leaves at nine—so I must write now. We are going to Mayence to-day, to see a house of our architect, Kraus, which is said to be very pretty and very English.

I paid Becker and his mother a visit yesterday. Their rooms are so nice, pictures and presents from

you and dear Papa in all directions, remembrances
of past, such happy, years!

Yesterday also I drove Baby out in my little
carriage. She sat on Christa's knees and looked
about her so much; she went to sleep at last.

November 17.

. . . Yesterday I was all the morning with Julie
Battenberg buying Christmas presents. To-day also
I am much occupied. We get up at seven, with
candles, every morning, as this is the best time for
doing all business, and breakfast at eight.

November 21.

. . . The Holstein question, I fear, will lead to
war, Fritz's* rights are so clear. And I am sure all
Germany will help him to maintain his rights, for
the cause is a just one.

I am sure, dear Mama, you are worried to death
about it, which is very hard, for you cannot undo
what once exists. *Anything* only to *avoid* war! It
would be a sad calamity for Germany, the end of
which no one can foresee.

* The late Duke Frederic of Augustenburg.

My Baby has this morning cut her first tooth, and makes such faces if one ventures to touch her little mouth.

To-day I am going to visit the hospital in the town, which is said not to be good or well looked after. I want to be able to do something for it and hope to succeed, for the people have plenty of money, only not the will. The Burgomaster and Gemeinderath [the Town Councillors], will meet me there.

I have just called into life what did not exist, that is, linen to be lent for the poor women in their confinements, and which I hope will be of use to them, for the dirt and discomfort is very great in those classes.

November 28.

. . . My visit to the hospital was very interesting, and the air was good, the place clean and fresh. There were few people dangerously ill there, and they looked well taken care of. Air and water are making their way into these places to the benefit of mankind.

I was so much distressed the other day; for the poor man who fell in our house has died. He was a soldier, and so respectable and industrious, not

above twenty-four.   This is already the second who
has died in consequence of a fall.

November 30.

A few words of love and affection from us both
on this dear day—the third anniversary of the commencement of all our happiness, which dear Papa
and you enabled us to form.

Those happy days at Windsor and those awful
days the year after! I assure you the season, the
days, *all* make me sad—for the impression of those
two years can never be wiped out of my mind.   I
can write but a few lines, as to-morrow we leave for
Amorbach, and to-day I go with Louis out shooting.
It is cold and fine, as it was two years ago.

Darling Mama, again and again we thank you
and beloved Papa for all your love to us at that
time.

Amorbach: December 2.

. . . We arrived here at half-past four yesterday
—after a bitter cold drive in an open carriage over
hard roads, all being frozen, since ten in the morning.   The country we came through was beautiful,
though all white, up and down hill all the way,
through many villages, through woods, &c.   The
house is large and comfortable, full of souvenirs

of dear Grandmama [Duchess of Kent], of Uncle
Charles.

I am so pleased to be with Ernest and Marie *
—it is a bit of home again.

December 8.

. . . Think, only yesterday evening at a concert
they played *Ruy Blas*, which I had not heard since
Windsor. The room, the band, dear Papa, all came
before me, and made my heart sink at the thought
that *that* belonged to the bright recollections of the
past! I cried all the way home. Such trivial things
sometimes awaken recollections more vividly, and
hurt more keenly, than scenes of real distress. I
am sure you know what I mean.

December 12.

. . . I must close—my tears fall fast, and I ought
not to make you sadder, when you are sad enough
already. Pray for me when you kneel at *his* grave
—pray that my happiness may be allowed to last
long; think of me when you kneel there where on
that day my hand rested on your and Papa's dear
hands, two years ago. That bond between us both
is *so* strong, beloved Mama. I feel it as a legacy
from him.

* Prince and Princess of Leiningen.

A great pleasure I have had in arranging a tree
for our good servants.   I bought all the things myself at the market, and hung them on the tree:
then I also got things for darling Louis.

. . . We all had trees in one large room in the
Palace, and our presents underneath it looked extremely pretty.   Uncle Alexander's five children
were there, and made such a noise with their playthings.

Baby had a little tree early at her Grandpapa
and Grandmama's, with all her pretty things.

Many thanks for the turkey-pie; we give a
dinner to-day in honour.

1864.

January 5.

. . . The cold here is awful. I skated yesterday, and to-day we are going to the pond at Kranichstein. (Very few people skate here—only one lady, and she very badly.) Baby only goes out for half an hour in the middle of the day, well wrapped up. It would not do to keep her quite at home, as she would become so sensitive when first taken out again. Of course when it is windy or too cold she stops in.

January 9.

I was aghast on receiving Bertie's telegram this morning announcing the birth of their little son. Oh, may dear Papa's blessing rest on the little one; may it turn out like dear Papa, and be a comfort and pride to you, and to its young parents! Your first English grandchild. Dear Mama, my heart is so full. May dear Alix and the Baby only go on well!

January 16.

. . . Baby says "Papa," "Mama," and yesterday several times "Louis." She imitates everything she hears, all noises and sounds; she gets on her feet alone by a chair, and is across the room before one can turn round. Her adoration for Louis is touching. She stops always, since the summer, alone in our room, so she never cries for Moffat [her nurse], and is very happy on the floor with her playthings. She is a very dear little thing and gets on very fast, but equally in all things, and is as fat as she was. It is so interesting to watch the progress and development of such a little being; and Baby is so expressive, she makes such a face when she is not pleased, and laughs so heartily when she is contented. She is more like a child of two years old a great deal.

January 30.

. . . These poor Schleswig-Holsteiners do what they can to liberate themselves from the Danish yoke, and to regain their lawful sovereign, Fritz. And why is England, who stands up for freedom of countries, who in Italy, where there was less cause, did what she could to liberate the country from her lawful sovereigns, to do what she can to prevent the Schleswig-Holsteiners from liberating themselves from a king who has no right over them, merely because they are unfortunate good-natured Germans, who allow themselves to be oppressed?

February 14.

. . . We have been in sledges to-day, and everybody drives about the town in them; it sounds so pretty, all the jingling bells.

. . . Shakespeare's words came home to one—

Uneasy lies the head that wears a crown.

Thank God, my husband has none! I thank the Almighty daily for our peaceful homely life, in which sphere we can do a good deal of good to our fellow-creatures, without having to mix in those hateful politics.

Our life is a very very happy one. I have nothing on earth to wish for, and much as I loved my precious Louis when I married him, still more do I love him now and daily; for his character is worthy of love and respect, and a better husband or father, a more unselfish and kind one, there does not live. His love for you, you know; and on our return how glad we shall be to be near you once more.

February 16.

Louis is in the Chamber to-day from nine till one, long enough at a stretch, and immediately after breakfast. We always breakfast at eight; then Louis sees the three officers who come every morning on his military business, then Westerweller and all others who have business. We usually walk before luncheon, which is at twelve; and often drive at two or three. At five we dine; at half-past six, theatre, four times a week, till half-past nine; then we take tea together, Louis reads to me and I work. On other week-days there are concerts or parties. We are often in our new house, and in the garden, arranging things and watching the progress. We also go to lectures here, and are much occupied, which makes the day pass so quickly.

March 1.

I have learned much since I married, and, above all, not to be dependent on others in my existence. To be able to make a bright and comfortable home for my dear husband is my constant aim; but even in this one often fails, for self constantly turns up, like a bad sixpence. Oh, how dear Papa spoke about that! His whole noble life was that one bright example of sacrificing himself to his duty. Dear, adored Papa! such goodness, such love, when

one thinks of it, must silence all complaints of petty
troubles in the mouths of his children and servants.
You, dear Mama, are the one who suffers the most,
though this awful loss has touched all; and to soothe
your grief and to help you lightens one's own.

March 5.

. . . Spring always makes me so *wehmüthig* [sad],
I don't know why; one longs for everything and
anything which is out of one's reach.

I will tell you of something I did the other day;
but please tell no one, because not a soul but Louis
and my ladies know of it here. I am the patroness
of the "Heidenreich Stiftung," to which you also
gave a handsome present in the beginning. The
ladies who belong to it go to bring linen to poor
respectable *Wöchnerinnen* [lying-in women], who
claim their assistance. They bring them food, and,
in short, help them. All cases are reported to me.
The other day I went to one incog. with Christa, in
the old part of the town—and the trouble we had
to find the house! At length, through a dirty
courtyard, up a dark ladder into one little room,
where lay in one bed the poor woman and her
baby; in the room four other children, the husband,
two other beds, and a stove. But it did not smell

bad, nor was it dirty. I sent Christa down with the children, then with the husband cooked something for the woman; arranged her bed a little, took her baby for her, bathed its eyes—for they were so bad, poor little thing!—and did odds and ends for her. I went twice. The people did not know me, and were so nice, so good and touchingly attached to each other; it did one's heart good to see such good feelings in such poverty. The husband was out of work, the children too young to go to school, and they had only four kreuzers in the house when she was confined. Think of that misery and discomfort!

If one never sees any poverty, and always lives in that cold circle of Court people, one's good feelings dry up, and I felt the want of going about and doing the little good that is in my power. I am sure you will understand this.

March 14.

My own dear precious Mama,

These words are for the 16th, the first hard trial of our lives where I was allowed to be with you. Do you recollect when all was over [death of the Duchess of Kent], and dear Papa led you to the sofa in the colonnade, and then took me *to you?* I took that as a sacred request from him to

love, cherish, and comfort my darling Mother to all
the extent of my weak powers. Other things have
taken me from being constantly with you; but nothing has lessened my intense love for you, and
longing to quiet every pain which touches you, and
to fulfil, even in the distance, his request.

Oh, darling Mama, were there words in which I
could express to you how much I am bound up
with you, how constantly my thoughts and prayers
are yours, I would write them. The sympathies of
our souls can only tell each other how tender my
love and gratitude to you is, and how vividly I feel
every new trial or new thing with you and for
you. . . .

I was with another poor woman, even worse off,
this morning, and on the third day she was walking
in the room and nearly fainted from weakness.
Those poor people!

March 26.

. . . Yesterday morning at nine we took the
Sacrament—all the family and congregation together. The others then stopped for the rest of
the service, till after eleven. I went home, and
returned for the English service at twelve. At half-
past six, in the Stadtkirche, Bach's "Passion" was
given.

April 5.

To-day is Victoria's birthday. What a day it was this time last year! Baby has her table in the room next to my sitting-room. Uncle Louis and the rest of the family expected to breakfast with us at twelve.

Munich: April 13.

· · · Between sight-seeing, and going to the Queen's room, and being with her, I have not a moment scarcely to rest or write. Yesterday we visited the whole Schloss full of frescoes, and the studios of all the famous painters—so interesting. How dear Papa would have enjoyed it! I was thinking the whole time what he would have thought of certain pictures, and how much he would have admired some. But at all times seeing things, and most of all pictures, is fatiguing.

Darmstadt: April 21.

. . . On Monday Louis goes into the country to shoot capercailzies [*Auerhähne*]. I accompany him part of the way, but stop at Schweinsberg with Christa's parents. The air is very good there, and we thought the country would do me good.

. . . We shall leave probably later [for England],

after or just before your birthday. We have a great deal to do in London for our house, for which I should want a week; and from Windsor to leave you for a whole week I should not like, and to go up constantly is rather tiring.

We go from Mayence to Rotterdam by steamer, from thence by rail to Antwerp, and then wait for good weather to cross, so that we shall be long under way, but quite easily and comfortably.

April 25.

. . . We shall leave the week of your birthday. Louis wishes us to have a full fortnight in London.

Darmstadt: May 14.

Many thanks for your letter, and above all for your great kindness about the ships, for which I thank you many times.

Christa and Becker wrote an account of the wedding,* so I won't write any more about it save that it went off very well and was very *vornehm* and well-arranged. . . .

* Of the Princess Anna of Hesse with the Grand Duke of Mecklenburg-Schwerin.

I have borne the fatigues well; but two days before, for two days and one night, I was very unwell. . . . Dr. Weber is a clever man, and is *viel-
seitig* [many-sided] in his views on medicine and
treatment of illnesses.   I think you will like him.

Baby runs alone through two rooms without
falling now: she learnt it in a week.   She will
amuse you so much.   Yesterday Louis drove me
and his two brothers in a break, and Baby went
with us much enchanted.

May 17.

. . . To-morrow afternoon Fritz and Anna leave.
To-day the town gives a large ball, to which we all
go, and before it there is a dinner at the Schloss.

May 21.

. . . It is excessively hot, which makes me so
tired and weak.   I am sure you suffered dreadfully
from the heat.

The parting from Anna three days ago was
dreadful; she so distressed, and her parents also....
They begin their old age alone, so to say, for there
are no children in their house any more.   It makes
us both very sad to leave them, and seems so un-
feeling; but we shall return to them soon.   What a

blessing that you have Beatrice and two brothers, still boys; and yet, for one alone what an anxiety!

Marlborough House: May 26.

Arrived here at half-past eleven, and quite rested. I at once write to you to thank you for your letter and for the great comfort of the ships. I feel so much better already from the air on the Rhine those two days, and the fresh sea air, that I have borne the journey this way with but little fatigue. I find Bertie and Alix both looking well, and the baby so pretty and dear.

I slept during the whole night passage, as I went to bed early. I had about twelve hours' sleep, which has completely set me up. Louis is paying visits. We have lunched, and in the afternoon Bertie and Alix have promised to call on Lady Augusta and Dean Stanley, and we join them. Aunt Cambridge and Mary we shall see afterwards.

[From May to August the Princess was in England on a visit to the Queen.]

Kranichstein: August 30.

. . . I have stood the journey well, though I am rather fatigued. It is very warm. Louis is off to

Jugenheim. I am to go there to-morrow, and it takes my whole day, as it is so far. I have seen none of the family yet. I was so distressed to part from dear Ernest and Marie, they were so dear and good all along the journey. The weather was beautiful and the passage good.

September 2.

. . . I am so glad that, from all accounts, everything went off so very well at Perth; * it must have been most trying to you, and yet satisfactory. We read all the accounts you kindly sent us with much interest.

. . . The Emperor [of Russia] with his second and third sons arrived yesterday. We saw him at the station at Darmstadt, but did not join them as the rest of the family did. We go to Jugenheim to-day and Baby with us, as little Serge,** who is just Beatrice's age, has such a passion for her. The children are very nice, the two older sons very big. Uncle Gustav is here, which makes me think of you here this time last year.

September 13.

. . . Two days ago we had intense heat, and

---

* The unveiling of a statue of the Prince Consort.
** Grand Duke Serge.

since great cold—the two extremes constantly, which is so unwholesome. The Emperor is very grateful for your message, and sends his best remembrance. . . . There were seven young men to dinner yesterday, and your glass was used for the first time and looked so pretty.

September 20.

. . . What you say about the poor sisters, and indeed of all the younger ones, is true. The little brothers and Beatrice are those who have lost the most, poor little things! I can't bear to think of it, for dear Papa, more peculiarly than any other father, was wanted for his children; and he was the dear friend, and even playfellow, besides. Such a loss as ours is indeed unique. Time only increases its magnitude, and the knowledge of the want is felt more keenly.

. . . I was yesterday in our little house, arranging and clearing out the rooms. We shall have very close quarters, but it will not be uncomfortable.

Where people are unselfish, loving, good, and industrious, like my dear Louis, I always feel a certain likeness beginning to grow up with our dear angel Father! Don't you? Oh, may we all only become like him! I struggle so hard, dear Mama,

in the many little trials I daily have, to become
more like him. My trials melt away when I think
of you, and I wish I were great and strong to be
able to bear some of your great trials for you. Dear
Mama, how I love you! how we both love you, and
would shield you with our love from all new blows
and trials, you know. God comfort you! My heart
is often too full to say all that is in it; to tell you
all my love and devotion, for your own precious
sake, and for dear Papa's, who left you as a legacy
to us all to love and to cherish for him.

September 23.

To-morrow Louis, I and my two ladies take the
Sacrament in the little church here. I wished much
to take it before my hour of trial comes. Dear
Louis read to me yesterday evening Robertson's
sermon on the "Sympathy of Christ."

We have fine autumn weather, and I am out as
much as I can. . . . I sleep well and breakfast
always at half-past eight; we dine at two, and take
supper at eight, then my ladies read aloud, and I
work or Christa plays, Louis reads his papers, &c.
To myself I read Lord Malmesbury's Memoirs,
which are very curious, and when Louis has time
he reads Froude to me.

Darmstadt: October 14.

We are at length here, in great disorder, and I have been waiting half an hour only for a pen to be found. I am tired and not very well. . . . Augusta [Lady Augusta Stanley] being with you I am very glad of, and she must be such a comfort to you, for, besides being such a friend, she has that peculiar charm of manner which all the Bruces possess.

October 29.

. . . To-morrow we expect Vicky and Fritz [Crown Prince and Princess of Prussia] for two hours, and later Bertie and Alix on their way back from Amorbach, for a few hours. I shall be delighted to see them.

October 31.

. . . Yesterday we had the pleasure of having dear Vicky and Fritz and baby here for two hours, the former well and in such good looks, as I have not seen her for long. The baby is a love, and very pretty. We were very glad after a year's separation to meet again, and Vicky was so dear and loving. I always admire her understanding and brightness each time I see her again; and Fritz so good, so excellent. Bertie and Alix we expect in a

day or two for a short visit. It is very cold, but
not unpleasant. I go out twice a day

Darmstadt: November 7.

. . . The little daughter * was but a momentary
disappointment to us, which we have quite got over.
We console ourselves with the idea that the little
pair will look very pretty together.

November 20.

. . . We are both very much pleased at the
arrangement about Brown and your pony, and I
think it is so sensible. I am sure it will do you
good, and relieve a little the monotony of your out-
of-door existence, besides doing your nerves good.
I had long wished you would do something of the
kind; for, indeed, only driving is not wholesome.
. . . I have had two drives, which have done me
good. . . . My mother-in-law has been kindness itself all along—so attentive and yet so discreet. I
can't be grateful enough. My good father-in-law
also. . . . Louis's mother is to be godmother, because it is customary here to ask someone of the

* The Princess Elizabeth was born on the 1st of November,
1864.

name the child is to receive to stand on the occasion. We liked Elizabeth on account of St. Elizabeth being the ancestress of the Hessian as well as the Saxon House.

November 26.

. . . We probably go to Carlsruhe on Wednesday, the only place we can well go to near by; we can't take an inn at Baden or anything of that sort, and we only go for a week or ten days at most. . . . I am very well and very careful; all people say I look better, and have more colour than I have had for long, and, indeed, I feel strong and well, and my fat Baby does perfectly, and is a great darling. Affie * and Louis and his brother are out shooting. The horrid weather has kept me in these three days.

November 29.

. . . I ought to mention the christening. My mother-in-law held Baby all the time, and it screamed a good deal. Victoria stood with us and was very good, only kneeling down and tumbling over the footstool every two minutes, and she kept whispering to me, "Go to Uncle's." I thought so much of

* Duke of Edinburgh.

the christening last year, when Victoria behaved
much better than her larger dark sister. Ella mea-
sured twenty-three and a half inches a fortnight
ago, and she had not grown then. Victoria, I believe, was twenty inches.

Carlsruhe: December 5.

. . . Dear Dr. Macleod is coming with Affie to
Darmstadt for the 14th. Vicky and Fritz will be
with us also. How kind of him to come, and it
has made Affie so happy, for he is so devoted to
him.

December 15.

I had not a moment to myself to write to you
yesterday, and to thank you for the kind lines you
sent me through dear Dr. Macleod. He gave us a
most beautiful service, a sermon giving an outline
of dear Papa's noble, great and good character, and
there were most beautiful allusions to you in his
prayer, in which we all prayed together most
earnestly for you, precious Mama!

We talked long together afterwards about dear
Papa, and about you, and though absent were very
near you in thought and prayer.

Dear Vicky talked so lovingly and tenderly of
you, and of how homesick she sometimes felt. She

was not with us on that dreadful day three years ago, and that is so painful to her. Dear Affie was, as we all were, so much overcome by all Dr. Macleod said. Vicky, Affie, Louis and myself sat in the little dining-room; he read to us there. Fritz had left early in the morning. The day was passed quietly and peaceably together, and I was most grateful to have dear Vicky and Affie with me on that day. My dear Louis wishes me to express to you how tenderly he thought of you and with what sympathy on this sad anniversary. Never can we cease talking of home, of you and of all your trials. God bless and comfort you, my own dear Mama!

1865.

. . . Thousand thanks for your dear words, and
for the wishes! I was thinking so much of you
and of home, when your letter came in. It made
me so happy! Darling Mama, I can feel so much
with and for you during these days. I was all day
on the verge of tears, for the very word *Neujahr*
brought Papa and Grandmama, and all at Windsor
as in former days, so vividly before me, it made
my heart ache! That bright happy past, particularly those last years, when I was the eldest at
home, and had the privilege of being so much with
you both, my own dearly loved parents, is a remembrance deeply graven, and with letters of gold,
upon my heart. All the morning I was telling
Louis how it used to be at home, and how we all
assembled outside your dressing-room door to scream
in chorus "*Prosit Neujahr!*" and to give to you
and Papa our drawings, writings, &c., the busy occupation of previous weeks. Then playing and re-

citing our pieces, where we often stuck fast, and
dear Papa bit his lip so as not to laugh; our walk
to the Riding-school [where the alms to the poor
were distributed], and then to Frogmore. Those
were happy days, and the very remembrance of
them must bring a gleam of sunshine even to you,
dear Mama. Those two dinners, when I was with
you both, were such happy evenings. I am so grateful I remained at home, and lost not a day of those
happy ones.

At eight this morning we two went to church;
at half-past three there was a large dinner at the
Schloss. I wore the bracelet with your pictures, as
I always do on all particular days, for I like to be
able to look at those dear faces.

January 2.

We mean to go out sledging. The cold, and
all the ground being white this last month, has
given me such bad eyes. I can do nothing of an
evening at all, and reading even by daylight makes
them so bad that they get quite red. The ladies
read to me, instead, all sorts of instructive things.
Louis has already found time to read through a
whole volume of the *Lives of the Engineers.* * You

* By Dr. Samuel Smiles.

could not have sent anything that would interest
him more. He thanks you so much for the pretty
New Year's wish also.

January 14.

Thousand thanks for your dear letter, for the
nice enclosure from Dr. Macleod, and for the
beautiful sermon by Dean Stanley. One remark
struck me as singularly applicable to dear Papa,
where he says: "To die is gain; to be no longer
vexed with the sight of evil, which they cannot
control," &c.—for dear Papa *suffered* when he saw
others do wrong; it pained that good pure spirit:
and though we long for him and want him, if we
could call him back—even you who want him so
much, I think, would pause before you gave vent to
the wish that would recall him. . . .

When trials come, what alone save faith and
hope in a blessed future can sustain one!

. . . You can't think how much I am interested
in every little detail of your daily life. Besides,
you know it cannot be otherwise. Please say kindest
things to Brown,* who must be a great convenience
to you.

---

* John Brown, the Queen's faithful personal attendant.

January 20.

. . . The more one studies and tries to understand those wonderful laws which rule the world,
the more one wonders, worships, and admires that
which to us is so incomprehensible; and I always
wonder how there can be dissatisfied and grumbling
people in this beautiful world, so far too good for
our deserts, and where, after our duty is done, we
hope to be everlastingly with those we love, where
the joy will be so great and lasting that present
sorrow and trouble must melt away before that sunshine.

January 23.

. . . We have rain and warm high wind, and
leave at four o'clock this afternoon. Ella has her
bath as a bed, and Victoria sleeps in the bassinet,
which is done up with chintz for the occasion. I
don't think they can catch cold. There is a stove
in the centre compartment besides. You can fancy
I feel shy going to Berlin into a perfectly new
society; and I have been so little out on the
whole since the year 1861. Marie Grancy * goes
with us.

Berlin: January 29.

. . . The journey went off very well, and we are

* One of the Princess's ladies in waiting.

so happy to be here. Vicky and Fritz are kindness itself, and Vicky so dear, so loving! I feel it does me good, that there is a reflection of Papa's great mind in her. He loved her so much, and was so proud of her. The King is, as always, very kind, and so pleased to see us here. Louis is very happy to meet his old comrades again, and they equally so to see him; and I am so glad that he can have this amusement at least, for he is so kind in not leaving me—and our life must be rather dull sometimes for a young man of spirit like him.

Berlin: February 4.

. . . I have not been sight-seeing anywhere, as it is too cold for that. We drive in a shut carriage, and then walk in the Thiergarten. We spend the whole day together, which is a great enjoyment to me, and of an evening we go out together. It is so pleasant to have a sister to go out with, and all the people are so kind and civil to us.

Sigismund* is the greatest darling I have ever seen—so wonderfully strong and advanced for his age—with such fine colour, always laughing, and so lively he nearly jumps out of our arms.

---

* Then the Crown Princess's youngest child.

This house is very comfortable, and Vicky is surrounded with pictures of you and dear Papa—near her bed, on all her tables—and such endless souvenirs of our childhood: it made me quite *wehmüthig* [sad] to see all the things I had not seen for seven years, and since we lived together as children—souvenirs of Christmases and birthdays from you both, and from dear Grandmama, from Aunt Gloucester, &c. It awakened a thousand old remembrances of happy past times.

Berlin: February 7.

. . . How much do I think of you now, the happy Silver Wedding that would have been, where you could have been surrounded by so many of us! Poor Mama, I do feel so deeply for you. Oh, may I be long, if not altogether, spared so awful a calamity!

Morning, noon, and night do I thank the Almighty for *our* happiness, and pray that it may last.

These lines are for the dear 10th,* though they will reach you on the eve; and they are to tell you from Louis and myself how tenderly we think of you on that day, and of darling Papa, who made

---

* The anniversary of the Queen's marriage.

that day what it was. It will be a day of great
trial to you, I fear. May the Almighty give you
strength and courage to bear it! I am sure the
dear sisters and brothers who are at home will try
to cheer you with their different loving ways—above
all, little Beatrice, the youngest of us all.

Louis goes to Schwerin to-morrow until Friday.
They wanted us to go together, but one journey is
enough at this time of the year.

Berlin: February 14.

. . . We leave next Saturday. I shall be so
sorry to leave dear Vicky, for she is often so much
alone. Fritz is really so excellent, it is a pleasure
to look at his dear good face; and he is worked so
hard—no health can stand it in the long run.

Berlin: February 17.

. . . This will be my last better from here, and
I only regret leaving here on account of parting
with dear Vicky and Fritz, whom we see so rarely,
and usually but for a short time. I have passed
such pleasant hours with dear Vicky: that is what
I shall look back to with so much pleasure and
satisfaction.

Darmstadt: February 21.

I write once more from our dear little home, which I find very cold; snow and ice everywhere still—it seems as if winter would never end. We accomplished our journey very well. Poor Vicky will miss us very much, I fear, in the many hours when she is alone, and which we spent together. Writing does not make up for it.

We give a large masked ball in the Palace at Fastnacht [Shrove Tuesday], which is to-day week. It is the first thing we do for the society, and I hope it will go off well. I found so much to do since my return that I can write no more.

Before closing I must mention, though, that yesterday evening I heard *Elijah* beautifully given. How I thought of dear Papa! Nearly every note brought back to mind observations he made about it. I thought I could see him, and hear his dear sweet voice turning round to me with quite watery eyes, saying, "Es ist doch gar zu schön" ["It is really quite too lovely!"]

Adored Papa! how he loved this fine music; the harmony in it seems like the harmony of souls, and Mendelssohn's music is so good, *fromm* [pious]—I mean, it makes one better to hear it. In the second part, in an air of Elijah towards the end, I found the part from which those beautiful responses are taken which Cusins* arranged, and which Papa liked so much.

March 4.

I have written to dear Tilla.** To think of home without her seems too sad, but I hope you will invite her sometimes. Everyone liked her in the house, she was so gentle and so kind. I shall never forget what I owe her, and I ever loved her most dearly. But she has never been the same again since 1861. It gave her a dreadful shock; she had such a veneration for darling Papa.

I hope this year we can show you our house, though it will not be far enough advanced for you to live in. For another year, I hope, we could make you so comfortable.

Darmstadt: March 6.

. . . I am reading at this moment a book by Herr von Arneth—the publication of letters from Maria Theresa to Marie Antoinette from 1770-80. I recommend it to you. The letters are short and interesting, and it would amuse you to take it up now and then, when you have a leisure moment.

---

* Master of the Queen's private band.
** Miss Hildyard, the Princess's former English governess.

The advice the Empress gives her daughter is so good; she was a very wise mother.

I have read and studied a great deal about the human body; about children—their treatment, &c. It interests me immensely. Besides, it is always useful to know such things, so that one is not perfectly ignorant of the reasons why doctors wish one to do certain things, and why not. In any moment of illness, before there is time for a doctor to come, one can be able to help oneself a little. I know you don't like these things, and where one is surrounded by such as dear Sir James [Clark] and Dr. Jenner,* it is perfectly unnecessary and pleasanter *not* to know a good deal. Instead of finding it disgusting, it only fills me with admiration to see how wonderfully we are made.

March 18.

My poor children have been confined to the house with dreadful colds and coughs. Victoria looks the most pulled, though Ella's cough was much more violent. I am happy to say that they are really better to-day; but we have snow every day, and that makes their recovery slower.

Yesterday night part of a large seed manufactory

* The Queen's own private physicians.

close by, near the artillery barracks, was burnt
down. The flames were enormous, but the damage
done was not great.

April 1.

. . . Since some days the snow is many feet
deep; one can get about in sledges, and Louis drove
me in one with four horses this morning. All intercourse by carriage is impossible, and this is very
inconvenient to the people in the country when
their "Post" cannot drive.

April 4.

I must begin by telling you how much pleasure
your telegram has given me. It is like my own
dear Mama to have her arms open for those who
want her kind support; and I can only repeat again,
that with you, and under your care alone, should I
like to leave my little ones so long! To them, indeed, it will in every way be an advantage, and I
shall be quite easy in leaving them there, where I
know they will have every care which can be given;
and it would make us both so happy to feel that in
this way we could give you some little pleasure.

Westerweller and Becker both wish very much
we may take this winter, D. V., for a journey. As
long as we have fewer servants and this small

house, it is easy to break up the whole establishment—later, this will be less possible. Louis has never been able to travel, and the advantage of seeing other parts of the world would be so great for him. Without me he would not do it; he says, alone he should not enjoy it. I urge this journey principally for his sake, and I hope you will support me in this. Since our marriage we have seen nothing, and all who can try to enlarge their knowledge. From books alone it becomes tedious and less advantageous.

Victoria is going to have a party of thirty children to-morrow in Prince Charles's rooms. The snow is thawing at length, and the sun is much too hot. The sudden spring is not pleasant. We have been out riding, and this evening I shall accompany Louis to the Schnepfenstrich [woodcock-shooting*], which in a fine evening, when the birds sing, is lovely. . . .

April 8.

. . . We shall be delighted to receive you in Kranichstein, and if you will send your suite all to Darmstadt we shall be able to arrange, though we have not one spare room anywhere, and I feel you

---

* This sport is practised in the evening twilight.

will be rather squeezed. How I look forward to meeting you again, after a year of separation, I can't say; and I am so glad that it will be under our roof that our joyful embrace will take place. As Uncle Louis is to have the Garter, may not Affie bring it to him *without* ceremony? He would like it so much better, if it can be so.

On the 17th Louis goes to Oberhessen to shoot capercailzies, and he deposits me and the children at Lich on his way, where he will join us again for my birthday.

Anna* was safely delivered of a little girl this morning, and is doing well.

April 15.

. . . We have been very anxious about Anna the last few days, for she has had fever since the 9th, and shivering still yesterday.

We have a great deal to do this morning, so I can write but shortly.

We have fine weather at length, and are out a great deal.

Yesterday we took the Sacrament at nine, and

---

* Prince Louis's sister, the Grand Duchess of Mecklenburg-Schwerin. She died on the 16th of April, 1865.

numbers of people with us. The service lasted till
past eleven, with a pause between.

April 18.

This is really a dreadfully sad death in our
family, and will be a blow to my dear parents-in-
law which will weigh them down for many a day.
They who lived so retired, and to whom the family
life was all—Anna the pet—"das Prinzesschen,"
whom they gave up so unwillingly, and with whom
they corresponded daily! It will be a blank in their
existence, which I can't bear to think of! Such
tender loving parents! My poor Louis was dreadfully distressed, though he feared the worst all along
since we knew that Anna had fever. He left with
Grolmann, having passed a dreadful morning. All
the old servants, tutors, friends, came crying to us.
Since he is gone I have passed sad lonely hours:
and poor old Amelung* comes and sits in my room,
sobbing that she should ever have lived to see this
day.

Yesterday morning I went to the Rosenhöhe and
picked flowers from Anna's garden, and wound a
large wreath, which I have sent to Louis to place
on her coffin. The three brothers feel it dreadfully

* Nurse of the Prince Louis and his brothers and sister.

—the first rent in the family circle is always hard
to bear, and she so young, so good, so happy! I
hear the poor little baby is nice.

Yesterday night Anna was taken into the Schlosskirche [Palace Chapel] upon Louis's arrival, after a
journey of twenty-seven hours. I hope he won't be
ill after all this *Gemüthsbewegung* [strain upon his
feelings], and fatigue always upsets him and makes
him sick, and he feels all so deeply and warmly.
It is so shocking. I can think of nothing else; and
I am very low and sad being so alone, and the
warm weather makes one unwell.

The poor Cesarewitch has passed a tolerable
night. I fear he is so reduced he can't get through
it. The Empress doats on this son, and he is so
like her. The poor Emperor has left for Nice.

                                        April 21.

Oh, it is sad, very sad! Life indeed is but a
short journey, on which we have our duty to do,
and in which joy and sorrow alternately prevail.
Anna was very good, very unselfish, and a true
Christian, with her gentle, humble spirit, and as
such she was loved and admired. What rare people
my parents-in-law and their children are, I can't
tell you—such childlike faith, such pure unselfish

love to each other; I really feel unworthy to belong
to them, and they are dear to me beyond description. As I have shared their joys, so with all my
heart do I share their sorrow, and fervently pray
for them! You will understand this, darling Mama.
From you I have inherited an ardent and sympathising spirit, and feel the pain of those I love as
though it were my own. To-morrow I have wished
that there should be in the Palace Chapel a funeral
service at the same time as the funeral at Schwerin,
and all the people here seemed pleased at my wish.
Bender, who taught her, confirmed her, and who
married her not a year ago in that very church, will
perform the service.

Poor Dagmar!* what a journey for her, poor
child! She begins her troubles early enough.

April 24.

. . . Many thanks for your kind letter, and for
all the kind wishes for my birthday. It will be sad
and quiet; but I hope my beloved Louis will arrive
to-night, and be with me again—such cause for joy
and thankfulness. When I have *him*, all sorrow is

---

* Princess Dagmar of Denmark, now Empress of Russia,
sister of the Princess of Wales.

turned into peace and happiness. Could I but know
you still had darling Papa at your side, how light
would my heart be! Once when we have all fulfilled our allotted duties, and overcome that dark
night, then, please God, we shall be together, never
again to part!

The sympathy of all does my sorrowing family
good, for it soothes so much! I had a few lines, so
tender, so full of faith, from my dear mother-in-law
to-day. Since Ella's birth I know to understand
and love her most dearly. She suffered dreadfully,
but no complaint passes her lips. She consoles her
husband, her son-in-law, and this, with prayer, en-
ables her to bear that which has almost broken her
heart.

April 29.

I thank you so much for your kind sympathising
letter. All my family are so grateful for all the
kindness and sympathy you have shown them on
this sad occasion.

To-day Uncle Louis arrives; on Monday the Emperor and Empress, and children. What a sad
meeting! They go to Jugenheim direct, where last
year they were so happy all together. I hear the
Empress is worn out, mind and body; and she in-
sists, instead of finishing her cure, on going in a

fortnight to St. Petersburg to meet the remains of her child. and to do him the last honours. Louis fears that it will be more than her feeble frame can endure. In the Greek Church, too, the night Masses are long and exhausting, and she is sure to wish to do all.

We spent my birthday as every other day, and the weather was heavenly. I am painting in oil now, and that interests me much. I find it much easier than water-colours.

I hope Affie will come to pay his respects to the Russians. If you send them a kind message through him, it would please them much.

May 2.

. . . How well I understand your compassion being alike for mourners in all positions of life. It is but right and natural, and I can't imagine one's feeling otherwise.

Seeheim: May 21.

. . . Yesterday the Emperor and Empress and children left. So sorry to see them go! God knows when we shall all meet here again. We have been so much together, and so intimately, that I have grown very fond of them, and am very sad at the thought of the long and uncertain separation. Dear little Arthur was here, looking very well. The wooded hills here are so nice to ride about on, and the country is very beautiful.

May 31.

I read serious books a great deal, and of a Sunday together we read out of Robertson's sermons. In the second series there is one, "The Irreparable Past," for young people, so cheering, so encouraging, so useful. Louis read it to me on his return from Schwerin after poor Anna's death. A short life indeed, and it makes one feel the uncertainty of life, and the necessity of labour, self-denial, charity, and all those virtues which we ought to strive after. Oh, that I may die, having done my work and not sinned with *Unterlassung des Guten* [omission to do what is good], the fault into which it is easiest to fall.

Our life being so quiet gives one much time for earnest thought, and I own it is discouraging to find how much one fails—how small the step of improvement is.

I suffer still so much, and so often, from rheumatism. I am taking warm soda-baths in the morning for it, and am rubbed afterwards with towels which have been dipped in cold water and then wrung out. It is not very pleasant.

. . . You know how very Scotch we both are.
Louis is devotedly attached to Scotland and his
Scotch friends. Do tell them so always. But now
I must tell you of yesterday. In the morning Affie,
we, and our suite, drove into town for the investi-
ture. At half-past three I drove with my ladies, a
Kammerherr [Chamberlain], Becker, &c., to the
Schloss, where Uncle Louis received us in *shorts!*
Then Affie and Louis in their whole Garter dress
arrived in a carriage with six horses and an escort.
Uncle Louis, before the throne, and the family,
Court, corps diplomatique, &c., received them. Affie
read in English the address, to which Uncle Louis
answered in German; then Affie buckled on the
Garter; then Louis helped him to put on ribbon,
cloak, &c., and fastened the sword on him, which
was no easy task; but they acquitted themselves to
perfection, and went out through the long Kaisersaal
backwards, bowing.

There was a large dinner afterwards, at which
your health was proposed by Uncle Louis, and in
return Affie gave his. You have made a happy
man, and he feels the honour—as he said to me in
English—"utmostly"; and he wishes me to repeat
once more how grateful he is to you. . . .

Affie did not return here last night; he slept at

12*

Darmstadt, and left this morning for Amorbach. To-day Uncle Ernest is coming to us, but only for one night. As we have again to go into town to fetch him, and it is very warm, I must close.

Seeheim: June 15.

. . . How it will amuse and please us to show the good excellent Scotchmen our home. It is a pleasure to hear of such devotion and attention to you as Brown's is, and indeed you are so kind to him, that his whole happiness must consist in serving so good a mistress.

I think you will be pleased to hear of a most kind and touching tribute which the Frauen [women] of Darmstadt have paid me. Two hundred and fifty have subscribed to have a splendid picture painted for me, by P. Weber, of Loch Katrine. I am to see it on Sunday. It is very much admired, and they sent the painter to Scotland to do it, thinking that something from my own country would please me most. Is it not kind of them? It has given me so much pleasure—but of all things the feeling which has prompted them to do it, as it shows me that, though I have been here so short a time, they have become attached to me, as I am with all my heart to my new home and country.

Ella crawls now, and is very strong; she has her first two teeth. Victoria is very wild, and speaks more German than English. I think her rather small, but other people say she is not. She goes out walking with her Papa before breakfast quite alone, with her hands in her pockets, and amuses him very much.

June 19.

Many thanks for your last letter from dear Balmoral. The parting from that lovely place must always be sad, and there is something in mountains which attaches one so much to that scenery.

Yesterday was a very trying day for my poor mother-in-law (her birthday), and she was very low, but, as all along, so resigned, so touching in the beautiful way she bears her grief; so unselfish with it, never wishing to make others sad, or to be less interested in their concerns than formerly.

Dear Mary Cambridge has been here, and we enjoyed her visit so much. We took her back to Frankfort to-day, where we gave her and Aunt Cambridge a luncheon in Uncle Louis's Palais.

June 21.

It is warm, but very windy and dusty here; we

were nearly blinded out riding yesterday evening.
I am reading that most interesting History of England by Pauli, in German, which commences with
the Congress of Vienna in 1815, and is, I believe,
very detailed and correct. It gives a sketch also of
the reign of George III., and is so well written one
can scarcely lay the book down. It is a part of a
work written by the best German professors on
England, Russia, Italy, France, Spain, and Austria
in those years, and I am reading them one after
another. They are thick books, and eight volumes.

Kranichstein: July 2.

We are all to go for four weeks to Switzerland,
beginning with Rigi Kaltbad. We go into the
mountains at once for the bracing air. On Saturday
until Tuesday we go to Baden for the christening of
the baby. We both are god-parents.

Kranichstein: July 10.

. . . Ella already says, since some time, "Papa"
and "Mama," and calls herself, and crawls, and is
very forward and merry—such a contrast to Victoria,
who is so pale and fair, and *now* thin, for Ella's
eyes are so dark blue, and her hair of such a rich

brown, that you would never take the little things for sisters. They are very fond of each other, and so dear together, that they give us much pleasure. I would not change them for boys, if I could; this little pair of sisters is so nice, and they can be such friends to each other.

I hope you will be comfortable here, but we are much annoyed not to be able to be there to receive you. None of the family will be here, save perhaps my mother-in-law with poor Fritz Schwerin,* who is expected then.

We mean to start on the 25th, and we go as private people, on account of the expense. We are only going to the Oberland, and shan't go very far about.

Kranichstein: July 17.

. . . It was 95° in the shade yesterday at eight in the morning, and I think the heat increases. Dr. Lyon Playfair lunched with us yesterday; he is so charming. To-morrow morning at five we go to Bonn for the day, and shall be there before ten. The heat is too great to go at any other time. We start next Tuesday evening, and on Wednesday shall be on the Rigi.

* Grand Duke of Schwerin, husband of Princess Louis' sister. He died 1882.

This morning at six o'clock we rode to the exercising—I on a new horse, for two hours and a half over sand without any shade.

Mary [Duchess of Teck] has been so kind as to give us a boat, which we expect shortly. It is to be christened "Mary Adelaide," after her.

July 24.

Many thanks for your letter, and for the sad account of Victoria Brand's* death. It is quite shocking, and she was my dearest friend of those contemporaries, and the one I saw the most of. "In the midst of life we are in death;" and the uncertainty of all earthly things makes life a real earnest, and no dream. Our whole life should be a preparation and expectation for eternity. Merry as she was, she was yet very serious and thoughtful; but what a loss she will be to her poor parents and husband!

I have made all arrangements for your comfort here. I own I do not like your coming here when we and the whole family are away—it looks so *odd!* I forgot to tell you, in answer to your question

---

* Daughter of M. Van de Weyer, the Belgian Minister Plenipotentiary in England. She had been thrown out of her carriage, and died from the effect of the injuries received.

about Ella's name, that she of course must be called
"Elizabeth," *entre nous* only "Ella," for she bears
my dear mama-in-law's name.

Rigi Kaltbad: August 1.

I am enchanted, delighted with this magnificent
scenery. Oh, how you would admire it! When I
am sketching, I keep telling Louis how much more
like you would make the things; one can always
recognise the places when you draw them.

We left Darmstadt at eight Wednesday morning,
the 26th, slept at Basel that night, and we got there
early enough to see the fine church in a thunder-
storm. The next day we only went to Lucerne, as
the weather was not fine enough to ascend the Rigi.
It was a lovely afternoon, and the lake of a marvellous green colour. The Pilatus was quite clear
for a few hours. The next morning we two, the
children, Moffat, Harriet the nursery-maid, Logoz
and wife, Jäger, and Beck, our whole party, started
in a very crowded steamer for Wäggis. Splendid
weather, though cloudy. We then, on horses and in
chairs carried by three or six men, made our ascent
along a winding, narrow, steep path, below rocks,
past ravines, where little châlets are situated, and
all over the green pasture cows and goats feeding

with bells round their necks. Westerweller was here when we arrived; he acts courier, and when we make long expeditions remains with the children. This is a very roomy hotel, crammed full of people, among them some odd Austrian ladies whom we see below walking on the terrace—very smart, and smoking. We two have been on mules with a guide —such a funny man, who was a soldier at Naples and was at the siege of Gaeta—on all the expeditions hereabout.

To-morrow we leave, and go till Monday to Buochs, on the other side of the lake; then to Engelberg, where Uncle Adalbert and his wife will be. The children are well; Victoria very troublesome, but Ella good and amiable as ever. As I am writing at the window, the clouds cover the lake and the lower mountains, and I can only see the quite high ones with glaciers, which are of such a splendid shape.

The colour of the Scotch mountains is, I think, finer; but here they are, first of all, so enormously high, and then such fine shapes, and the mountains are studded with trees and rocks down below, and of a green colour.

The air is very light and cold, but the sun intense. We are going off for the day again on our mules, so I must close. Of course many funny incidents take place, which I reserve to tell you when we meet.

I do hope the heat will be over for your journey, and that it will be fine when you are at our dear Kranichstein. Marie Grancy will be there to receive you, and do anything which is required.

Engelberg, Hôtel Titlis: August 8.

These lines I send by Becker, and hope you will receive them at Kranichstein. . . . I hope you found all you wanted in the rooms, and that the meals were as you like them. I ordered all, and wrote all down before leaving, as I know what you like.

We were for some days at Buochs, a very pretty village; and we lived in three detachments in different common Swiss houses, very comfortable on the whole, but not smelling very nice, so that I could scarcely eat while we were there.

Yesterday morning, in a very funny two-seated carriage with one horse, we left, the children and servants following in a bigger carriage. A nearly four hours' drive through the most beautiful scenery, up a narrow valley through which the Aa runs, brought us here. The last two hours are a steep ascent on the side of a precipice; beautiful vegetation through the wood all the way upwards; view on the high mountains with snow and glaciers close by. On coming to the top, there is a narrow and lovely green valley studded with peasants' cottages, and in the centre a Benedictine Abbey, near which our hotel is situated. The valley is of very green grass; the tops of the mountains quite rocky, with snow. Lower down, and skirting the valley, which is quite shut in by the hills, fine trees; several very high waterfalls, in the style of the Glassalt (near Balmoral), only much higher. This Alpine valley is said to give the most perfect idea of a Swiss valley up in the mountains. One can ascend the Titlis; but it is said to be dangerous, so we shan't attempt it. We are very careful, and Louis won't undertake anything risky. The scenery seen from the carriage merely is so splendid that one may well be content with that. Unfortunately, to-day it pours, and it is very cold. The children are very well. The journey has really done Victoria good, and she begins to have an appetite, which with her is a very rare thing.

The next place we go to is Meyringen. We mean to ride there over the Joch Pass, but the children must go back the same way to get round, as there is no other way out of this valley. We will leave them then with Westerweller, and go to the Grindelwald, Interlaken, &c.; and then return home by the 29th, probably. The children are living in a cottage here also.

Pension Belle Vue, Tracht bei Brienz: August 14.

. . . Our ride from Engelberg over the Joch Pass to Meyringen was quite beautiful; but a worse way than any we have ever been out on in Scotland. We were eleven hours on the road, and the sun was very hot, and the walking on these steep bad paths made one still hotter; but we enjoyed it very much, and I never saw anything grander or more magnificent. . . . I have made little scribbles on the way. . . . To-day we two with two horses were to have walked and ridden to the Grindelwald, over the Rosenlaui glacier, and to have gone on the next day to Interlaken, but the weather is so bad that it is impossible, and, not being satisfied with the prices, &c., at the hotel of Meyringen, we came on here, an hour's drive, near to the beautiful falls of the Giessbach, which we saw on Sunday. . . . The weather will determine whether we can make an expedition to-morrow.

We shall be home on Friday by Thun and Basel, where we sleep. What day are we to be at Coburg, and for how long exactly? I believe only two or three days.

The white heather is from above Engelberg,
near Brienz.

I have this instant received your dear letter from
Kranichstein, and, though only just returned from
an expedition to the Rosenlaui glacier, I sit down
at once to thank you with all my heart for such
dear lines. How glad I am all was comfortable,
and that you were pleased with your day in our
nice Kranichstein! I am glad you missed us a
little. . . . But I must tell you of to-day. We drove
to Reichenbach, close to the falls, took a guide and
horses, and in two hours by a steep stony path got
to Rosenlaui. The view on the Wetterhorn, covered
with snow, and on the Wellhorn, which is a rugged
rock on the other side of it, the white sparkling
glacier, is quite beautiful. The shapes and immense
height of the mountains are so imposing. I look,
admire, wonder; one can't find words to express
what one feels. How you would admire the scenery!
Papa was so fond of it all.

These will be my last lines until we meet. We
returned here well, having unfortunately, though,
much rain from Interlaken to Basel. At Thun we

were in the same hotel as Blanche* and Mademoiselle Bernard,** and to-morrow we expect Uncle Nemours, Marguerite,*** and Alençon,† whom we asked to dinner on their way to Frankfort. I am mostly at the Rosenhöhe with my mama-in-law, as she is quite alone. I was in town with her, and read to her this morning; she is ever so dear and kind. I do love her *so much*. Ever since Ella's birth we have been drawn so closely to each other, and I admire her also now that I know and understand her. There is so much beneath, so much *Gemüth*, tenderness, and delicacy of feeling. It is indeed a blessing to have such people as they are for parents-in-law.

September 1.

Uncle George was here yesterday. Vicky remains with us till the 5th, and it gives me so much pleasure to be able to repay her for her hospitality this winter.

Kranichstein: September 8.

. . . After having missed the train they intended to come by, Bertie and Alix arrived at three o'clock.

* Youngest daughter of Duc de Nemours.
** Governess of Princess Blanche.
*** Eldest daughter of Duc de Nemours.
† Second son of the same.

They dined with us. Louis then took him to the theatre, and I drove her about.

My poor father-in-law's throat is very bad, and gives him much pain. I am really very anxious about him.

We leave to-morrow afternoon at four, and shall spend the following day at Ostend, embarking in the evening. Till the end of the week we intend stopping in town, and if Bertie and Alix remain longer we shall leave by the limited mail (for Balmoral).

Inverness: October 8.

This is a very fine town, and the country is very beautiful. We took a walk this morning, and shall drive this afternoon. It was thought better not to go to a kirk, as the people seemed to look out for us.

Again a thousand thanks for having arranged this nice journey for us, which we enjoy so much. I thought so much of you and dear Papa yesterday during our ride.*

Sandringham: November 16.

. . . I am pleased that the children are well under your roof. I know they have all they can

---

* See *Leaves from a Journal*—Grantown, 1860.

want. Bertie had such bad toothache yesterday: Louis also a little; the cold air must be the cause, for it is so sharp here.

Alix and I practise together for an hour of an evening. . . . Alix drove me down to the sea the other day, and a most alarming drive it was, for the horses pulled, and, to our astonishment, the coachman suddenly alighted between us, with his feet in the air, from the back seat, and caught hold of the reins—it was too funny. I hope to be near you again on Saturday.

Darmstadt: November 28.

. . . I find my father-in-law looking better, I am happy to say, though far from strong; and alas! one of his lungs is affected. Though, with care, one can guard him from evil consequences, still of course it is an anxious thing. All the family are very grateful for your kind messages, and send their respects to you.

. . . The children are very well, and Victoria said to my mother, "Meine Grossmama, die Königin, has got a little vatch with a birdie," and she is always speaking of all at Windsor, but principally of the things in your room. I am so glad that you are pleased with the children's picture. I admire it so much.

Darmstadt: December 5.

Many thanks for your letter received yesterday, with the account of Lenchen's *Verlobung* [betrothal]. I am so glad she is happy, and I hope every blessing will rest on them both that one can possibly desire.

I had a letter from Marie Brabant* two days ago, where she says dear Uncle's [King Leopold's] state is hopeless; but yesterday she telegraphed that he was rather better. What a loss it would be if he were to be taken from us, for his very name and existence, though he takes no active part in politics, are of weight and value.

Yesterday I was painting in oils, and I copied my sketch of the Sluggan, and, if it be in any way at all presentable and fit to give, I will send it to you. I hope it won't be very Chinese, for our sketches had a certain likeness to works of art of that country. Louis is very busy here. He has begun his military duties; he has the command and *Verwaltung* [administration] of the Cavalry Brigade. To-day he has to go to the Chamber, and he is going to attend the different offices—home department, finances, justice, &c.—so as to get a knowledge of the routine of business. . . .

* Duchess of Brabant.

Darmstadt: December 8.

We are so grieved and distressed at dear Uncle Leopold's* alarming state, and have given up all hope, the accounts are so bad. Oh, were there but a chance for you, or for any of us who love him so dearly, to be near him during his last hours!

December 11.

Many thanks for your letter. Alas, alas! beloved Uncle Leopold is no more! How much for you, for us, for all, goes with him to the grave! One tie more of those dear old times is rent!

I do feel for you so much, for dear Uncle was indeed a father to you. Now you are head of all the family—it seems incredible, and that dear Papa should not be by your side.

The regret for dear Uncle Leopold is universal —he stood so high in the eyes of all parties; his life was a history in itself—and now that book is closed. Oh, it is so sad, and he is such a loss! I am almost glad this sorrow has fallen into those days already so hallowed by melancholy and precious recollections. How I recollect every hour, every minute of those days. In thinking of them

* King of the Belgians.

one feels over again the hope, the anxiety, and
lastly the despair and grief of that irretrievable loss.
The Almighty stood by you and us, and enabled us
to bear it, for I always wonder that we lived through
that awful time.

The future world seems so like a real home, for
there are so many dear ones to meet again. There
is something peculiarly sad in the death of the last
one of a large family—to feel that none is left to
tell of each other, and of their earlier life, which
the younger ones could know only through their
lips.

December 15.

Many thanks for your letter. I was so anxious
to hear something of our beloved Uncle's end; it
seems to have been most peaceful.

There will be many Princes at Brussels, I believe.

How much I thought of you and of dear Papa
on the 14th! Dear Louis leaves me this afternoon.
He will reach Brussels at five to-morrow morning,
and remain over the Sunday.

The accession of a new King and the honours
that have at once to be paid are so painful, following so closely on the death of one we have loved

and known in that position. As the French say:
"Le Roi est mort. Vive le Roi!"

December 20.

. . . I was sitting up for Louis till half-past
eleven with Countess Blücher—who leaves to-day,
and has spent a few days with me—when he and,
to my astonishment, Bertie also, came into the room.
The next day, alas! he had to leave again at four;
but still, short as his stay was, it was a token of his
constant love for me, and it touched me very much,
for I ever loved him so dearly.

Everything went off well at Brussels, as you will
have heard. The more I realise that we shall never
see beloved Uncle Leopold again, the sadder I grow.
He had, apart from all his excellent qualities, such
a charm as I believe we shall seldom find again.

The dear Countess is well. We made the dining-room into a bedroom for her, and we dined
downstairs. I was so afraid of her getting cold, if
she lived out of the house.

Darmstadt: December 24.

. . . How I wish beloved Uncle were brought to
Windsor to rest there as he had wished! I wondered
so much that everything had taken place at Laeken,
knowing that dear Uncle had wished it otherwise.

Uncle Louis wishes me to thank you once more for the Christmas eatables, and my mother-in-law likewise for the lovely little frame and photograph. They are both much touched by this kind attention on your part.

Christmas Day.

. . . To me Christmas is always sad now, and for Louis and his family it was so likewise this year; my parents-in-law felt it very much. We went to the Military Church at eight this morning. It is the service we like best; but it was bitterly cold, everything snow white.

I hope my little picture, though very imperfect, found favour in your eyes. It gave me such pleasure doing it for you, thinking of you and our expedition the whole time I was doing it.

December 30.

This is my last letter this year. In many ways a happy one has it been, though it has deprived us of many dear and near ones. Each year brings us nearer to the *Wiedersehen* [reunion with the dead], though it is sad to think how one's glass is running out, and how little good goes with it, compared to the numberless blessings we receive. Time goes incredibly fast.

Every earnest and tender wish from us both is yours, dear Mama, for this coming year with its expected events. May God's blessing rest on this new union which is to be formed in our family, and may dear Lenchen be as happy as all those who loved her can wish! I am so sorry to think that I shall probably not see her again until she is married; but I am glad for her sake that the *Brautstand* [the betrothal period] is not to be long.

I send you a locket with Ella's miniature, which I hope will please you.

1866.

I am at the head of a committee of ladies out of the different classes of society to make a large bazaar, in which all the country is to take part, for the Idiot Asylum. It is very difficult—all the more as I have never had anything to do with such things in my life. . . . I wanted, for the first public thing I undertake, to take in all principles, and my mother-in-law has given her name to it. I have chosen the committee out of different sets—half *adelig* [people of rank], half *bürgerlich* [of the citizen class], and all these ladies, half of whom I did not know before, come and sit in my small room and discuss— and, as yet, do not disagree.

. . . The people here are so much pleased that my Louis takes such active part in all his duties— military and civil—for he attends the different offices, and as General, I hear, he keeps great order

where there was until now disorder and great abuse
of power.   Of course, I see him much less, and
some days scarcely at all.

On the 14th we go to Gotha for about a fortnight, without the children.

Gotha: January 19.

Dear Uncle and Aunt are well, and we are very
happy here, for they are always kindness itself to
us.   Uncle looks very well, but he grows very stout,
I think.   We saw the *Braut von Messina* [Schiller's]
so well given two nights ago.   I thought so much of
dear Papa, who admired it greatly; and Uncle Ernest told me he had it given for you, when you first
came here.

Gotha: January 22

Our Quaker acquaintances have sent me a great
deal for the bazaar, and an old gentleman who
heard of it, 100*l.*!   I could not believe my eyes.
They are always so generous: and, hearing of my
undertaking a work of this sort, they sent me this
spontaneously.   Is it not kind?

Darmstadt: February 1.

It is spring weather here altogether—quite warm
when one comes out of the house.   It is so un-

natural. The children enjoy it, and are out a great deal, looking so well and strong: I wish you could see them. The little one is growing up to her sister very fast, and actually wears the frocks Victoria wore last year. I wish you could hear all the extraordinary things Victoria says. Ella is civil to all strangers—excepting to my mother-in-law, or to old ladies. It is too tiresome. There is a large ball given by the officers at their Casino to-night, to which we must go. It will be crowded and hot. Our house gets on tolerably. The housekeeper, a Berlinerin, comes on the 20th, and we are told that we can go into the house next month. I can't help doubting it, and I regret leaving this nice little house, where our first happy years have been spent. I am so glad that you have at least been in the new house, so that I can always think that you are no stranger to it, which makes me like it much better.

February 10.

. . . I am happy to think you are quiet at Osborne after all you had to go through. The emotion and all other feelings recalled by such an event must have been very powerful and have tried you much.* It was noble of you, my darling Mama,

---

* The opening of Parliament by the Queen for the first time after the death of the Prince Consort.

and the great effort will bring compensation. Think
of the pride and pleasure it would have given
darling Papa—the brave example to others not to
shrink from their duty; and it has shown that you
felt the intense sympathy which the English people
evinced, and still evince, in your great misfortune.

How to-day recalls those bright and happy
former years? There is no cloud without a silver
lining, and the lining to the black cloud which
overshadows your existence is the bright recollection of the past blending into the bright hope of a
happy future; a small part of it also is the intense
love of your children and nation, which casts a
light around you which many live to enjoy and
admire, and which few—if any—possess like you.
I wish I could have sent a fine nosegay of orange
blossoms for to-day, but they could not have arrived
fresh, so I gave it up.

Louis sends his tenderest love, and wishes me
to say how much his thoughts with mine are to-day
constantly with you. He is very industrious, and
has a great deal to do now, and, I hear, does all
very well.

Darmstadt: February 15.

How dear of you to have written to me on the
10th—a day of such recollections! That last happy

wedding-day at Buckingham Palace, how well I remember it, and all the previous ones at Windsor, when we all stood before your door, waiting for you and dear Papa to come out. You both looked so young, bright, and handsome. As I grew older, it made me so proud to have two such dear parents! And that my children should never know you both together—that will remain a sorrow to me as long as I live.

March 16.

How trying the visit to Aldershot must have been, but it is so wise and kind of you to go. I cannot think of it without tears in my eyes. Formerly that was one of the greatest pleasures of my girlhood, and you and darling Papa looked so handsome together. I so enjoyed following you on those occasions. Such moments I should like to call back for an instant.

Our house here is quite empty, and the *déménagement* creates such work. To-morrow night we sleep for the first time in the new house.

March 17.

I write from our dear little old house. May dear Papa's and your blessing rest on our new home, as I am sure it will! It is full of souvenirs of you both—all your pictures, photographs of dear brothers and sisters and home. It reminds me a little of Osborne, of Buckingham Palace, a little even of Balmoral. Could I but show it to darling Papa! If I have any taste, I owe it all to him, and I learned so much by seeing him arrange pictures, rooms, &c.

At half-past seven we go into our house to-night. Bender is to say a prayer and pronounce a blessing, when we with all our household are assembled in hall; only Louis's parents and William besides ourselves. Yours and dear Papa's I pray to rest on us.

March 20.

That [the death of the Duchess of Kent] was the commencement of all the grief; but with darling Papa, so full of tenderness, sympathy and delicate feeling for you, how comparatively easy to bear, compared to all that followed!

. . . We are very comfortably established here, and I can't fancy that I am in Germany, the house and all its arrangements being so English. When can we hope once to have you here? Of course *that* is the summit of our wishes. Your rooms are on the east side and very cool—as you always go abroad when it is hot, and suffer so much from the

heat. I shall die of it this year, as my rooms are
to the west.

March 24.

. . . Our Grand-Uncle of Homburg has just
died, so that Homburg falls to Uncle Louis now.
But all the things of the Landgravine Elizabeth go
to Princess Reuss, and her [Aunt Elizabeth's *]
rooms are full of beautiful miniatures, oil-paintings,
and ornaments *en masse*, like Gloucester House.

I shall be so glad to see dear Affie. His rooms
are to be ready by this evening. The house is
very comfortable, but the weather is awful—wind,
rain, and sleet. In spite of it the house is so
cheerful.

Dear Lady Frances Baillie was with me on
Thursday, so dear and charming.

April 2.

. . . We are living in such a state of anxiety
and alarm. War** would be too fearful a thing to
contemplate—brother against brother, friend against
friend, as it will be in this case! May the Almighty

---

* Princess Elizabeth of Great Britain and Ireland, Princess
Alice's grant-aunt.
** War between Prussia and Austria was now imminent.

avert so fearful a calamity! Here, at Mayence and
Frankfort, it will begin, if anything happens, as
there are mixed garrisons; and we must side with
one against the other. For Henry,* who is still
here, it is dreadful. He can't desert at such a moment, and yet if he should have to draw his sword
against his country, his brothers fighting on the
other side! Fancy the complications and horrors
of such a war!

For Vicky and Fritz it is really dreadful; please
let me hear by messenger what you hear from
them. I am sure you think of us in these troubled
times. What would dear Papa have said to all
this? I long to hear from you, to know that your
warm heart is acting for Germany.

March 26.

. . . The dear old Queen Marie Amélie ** is
gone to her rest at last, after a long and so stormy
a life! Claremont is now also altered. How sad
those constant changes are! It reminds one again
and again that we are on a journey, and that the
real home is elsewhere. All those who work hard
and love their fellow-creatures meet again, and the

---

* Prince Henry of Hesse, Prince Louis' second brother.
** Widow of King Louis Philippe.

thorny path will be forgotten which leads to the happy meeting. I sincerely mourn for the dear Queen, and she was so kind to me always. I am glad she was one of Victoria's godmothers.

April 7.

... Our Bazaar goes off wonderfully: 7,000 florins the first day, and to-day again a great deal. Affie was invaluable in arranging, selling, and assisting in every way. There have been crowds these two days, as in England: something quite unusual for the quiet inhabitants of this place. They have shown so much zeal and devotion that I am quite touched by it, as I am more or less a stranger to them.

April 25.

Thousand thanks for your dear lines, and for the money and charming bas-relief of you, which I think very good. I thought so much of former birthdays at home in Buckingham Palace. They were so happy. We did nothing in particular; merely dined at Kranichstein with Uncle Louis in the afternoon. It was warm and fine.

May 3.

... The prospect of war seems to be nearing realisation. It will be so dreadful if it does. God

be with us, if such a misfortune befall poor Germany!
These prospects have already done much harm to
trade. The large manufactories send away their
superfluous workmen, and they sell next to nothing.
Most unpopular amongst high and low, and amongst
people of all opinions, this civil war will be. . . .

I have made all the summer out-walking dresses,
seven in number, with paletots for the girls—not
embroidered, but entirely made from beginning to
end; likewise the new necessary flannel shawls for
the expected. I manage all the nursery accounts,
and everything myself, which gives me plenty to do,
as everything increases, and, on account of the
house, we must live *very* economically for these
next years.

If there is a war then, and Louis is away, what
shall I do? This is my constant dread and appre-
hension. As long as he comes home safe again—
that is all I shall think of. Please God to spare
me that fearful anxiety, which weighs on me now
already; for he, having only a brigade, could not
keep out of danger, like Fritz* in Schleswig.

I put my trust wholly in the Almighty, who has
watched over and blessed our life so richly thus far
—so *much, much* more than I ever deserved, or can

* Crown Prince of Prussia.

deserve; and He will not forsake us in the hour of need, I am sure.

These dangerous times make one very serious and anxious; the comfort of faith and trust in God, who does all well and for the best, is the only support. Life is but a pilgrimage—a little more or a little less sorrow falls to one's lot; but the anticipation of evil is almost as great a suffering as the evil itself, and mine always was an anxious nature, so I cannot banish the thoughts which all the dreadful chances of war force upon one.

May 7.

. . . I am so sorry for poor Louise and Beatrice, and whooping cough is a nasty thing, though I wish we could complain of that as our sufferings here. Anxiety, worry without end!

Uncle Alexander returned from Vienna two days ago. The Emperor, Uncle Alexander Mensdorff, all frantic at being forced into war, but fearing now no more being able to prevent it. Cannot the other three Powers interfere and step between at this dangerous crisis—proposing a Congress, or anything, so as to avert this calamity?

Henry, who was here on six weeks' leave, as he and Uncle Louis were to have gone to Russia (which now, of course, they won't do), had suddenly to return to Bonn, as his regiment is made *mobil*. Uncle Alexander receives the command of the 8th Armee-corps, which I suppose and hope will be stationed somewhere near here, as Louis is in that, and *is to go*. He means to go to Berlin this afternoon for a day to see Fritz, and tell him how circumstances now force him to draw his sword against the Prussians in the service of his own country. The whole thing is dreadful, and the prospect of being left alone here at such a moment (for all our people, nearly, will accompany Louis) is dreadful! If I were only over my troubles I should not be so anxious, so nervous and unhappy, as I must say the anticipation of all these dreadful things makes me. Could I follow in the distance! But now that is impossible, and I have not a single older married person near me. When dear Louis goes, of course Westerweller goes too. I still pray and hope against hope that there may be no war; even if all the troops are assembled, I hope that the other Powers will interfere, and not look on whilst these brothers cut each other's throats. It is such an unnatural, monstrous war!

May 18.

. . . How glad I am to hear that Lord Clarendon is still hopeful! Here as yet, though there is no distinct reason for it, save the repugnance of all to this civil war, all still hope to avoid the war. Every day we have occasion to hear how the Prussians detest this war—army and all—and there are constant rows, with the Landwehr in particular. Men of forty, who have families and homes to look after, are taken away with their sons; and those who have horses are also taken, with their horses: so that the wife and children sit at home, unable to do anything for their land. It is ruining numbers, and murmurs get louder and louder. A revolution must break out if this continues. . . . I do pray *most fervently* that the King will listen to the just advice, in no way derogatory to his dignity, of placing the hated question of the Duchies before the Confederation; but I fear he won't. If he would only listen to that advice and disarm, all Germany would do it at once—only too gladly—forgetting all the losses in the happiness of peace restored. Forgive my stupid letter, but we live really so in the midst of these affairs, on which our existence will turn, that I can think of nothing else.

Austria can't hold out much longer, and the country is getting very violent against the King and Bismarck. The Emperor is less able to concede and keep peace.

Now good-bye, dearest Mama. We are so grate-

ful to you for taking the children, if anything comes
to pass.

May 22.

. . . Anything you hear of Vicky and Fritz, will
you write it to me? . . . The cloud grows blacker
every day, and the anxiety we all live in is very
great. But I ought not to write to you to-day of
such gloomy things, which, thank God, you only see
and hear of from the other side of the water.

May 25.

. . . The Duke and Duchess of Nassau were
here yesterday. They, like me, are in such an unpleasant position, should it come to blows, which I
still hope may be averted—for why should we
harmless mortals be attacked?

. . . We shall be beggars very soon, if all goes
on as it promises to do; it is quite dreadful, and
the want of other people (and dissatisfaction) increases. . . . I have ordered a good travelling-bag
for Louis, for much the same reason that some
people take out an umbrella in fine weather to keep
off the rain, and this is to be against a war. . . . I
have a sort of *Ahnung* [presentiment] that it won't
come to the worst—for us at least—and here we

shall keep so quiet, only on the defensive, if attacked.

May 28.

. . . There seems a little chance of the dreadful
prospects being bettered. How I do pray it may
be the commencement of a better time; and that, if
peace be established, it may be so *firmly*, so that
one may not live in the daily dread of new quarrels
re-opening between the two countries. . . .

June 8.

. . . How precious are your words of love and
sympathy and the hope you still hold to, that war
may somehow be averted! It does me good to
hear it; and I know how much, and how lovingly,
your thoughts dwell with dear Vicky and with me
during this time of trial. . . .

June 13.

. . . I fear if the Bund orders the mobilisation,
and goes against Prussia, our troops will be the first
to go, and then Louis may get orders to be off any
day. It is too dreadful! I live in such dread that
he may have to go just before, or at the very moment of, my confinement. . . .

I hope Scotland will do you good. Please God,

when you return matters may be better. If Austria and Prussia would only fight out their quarrel together; but the latter has taken refuge with the Bund now, because she wanted it.

Darmstadt: June 15.

. . . The serious illness of poor little Sigismund* in the midst of all these troubles is really dreadful for poor Vicky and Fritz, and they are so fond of that merry little child.

We have just received the news that the Prussians have crossed our frontier and established themselves at Giessen. The excitement here is dreadful, and it is very difficult to keep people back from doing stupid things—wanting to attack, and so on, which with our force alone would be madness.

Louis—as always—remains quiet; but we live in a perpetual fever, alarms being sent, being *gehetzt* [stirred up] from Vienna, as they want the Bund to go with them at once. It is a dreadful time. I anticipate it will be the close of the existence of the little countries. God stand by us! Without the civil list Uncle Louis and the family are beggars, as all the private property belongs to the country.

---

* Son of the Crown Prince and Princess of Prussia. See *ante*, p. 164.

It is so kind of dear Lady Ely to offer to come.
I shall be very glad of it, for from one day to another I don't know what Louis' duties may be; and,
when I am laid up, it is so pleasant to have someone who can write to you.

June 18.

These lines I send by our children, whom you
so kindly will take charge of—alas, that the times
should be such as to make this necessary! In your
dear hands they will be so safe; and if we can give
you a little pleasure in sending them, it would be
a real consolation in parting from them, which we
both feel very much.

The state of excitement here is beyond description. Troops arriving, being billeted about—
all will be concentrated from here to Frankfort.
Two days ago the Bund telegraphed for Uncle
Alexander to come, as the Prussians were ad-
vancing; we, of course, were all unprepared, and
the confusion and fright were dreadful; but, thank
God, they retreated again, when they got wind that
troops were assembling. . . .

June 24.

. . . The state of affairs is awful; perpetual frights
and false news arrive. The Prussians are coming

from Wetzlar or Bingen; all the bustle and alarm
for necessary defence; it is really dreadful. Louis'
chief has his staff at Frankfort. Louis' cavalry
brigade is there likewise, so he has his adjutant, &c.,
there, and does his work early in the morning at
Frankfort, returning here in the afternoon, which
has been kindly allowed on account of me. I remain here, of course, as near dear Louis as I can;
and now that the children are gone, I have only
myself to look after. . . . I have not the least fear,
but my anxiety about Louis will be very great, as
you can imagine. . . . Collections are already being
made for the hospitals in the field, and the necessary
things to be got for the soldiers. Illness and wounds
will be dreadful in this heat. Coarse linen and rags
are the things of which one can't have enough, and
I am working, collecting shirts, sheets, &c.; and now
I come to ask, if you could send me some old linen
for rags. In your numerous households it is collected
twice a year and sent to hospitals. Could I beg for
some this time? It would be such a blessing for
the poor Germans; and here they are not so rich,
and that is a thing of which in every war there has
been too little. Lint I have ordered from England
by wish of the doctors; and bandages also they
wished for. If you could, through Dr. Jenner, pro-
cure me some of these things, I should be so grate-

ful. . . . Four dozen shirts we are making in the
house.   Every contribution of linen, or of patterns
of good cushions, or any good bed which in the
English hospitals has been found useful, we should
be delighted to have. . . . For the moment the
people beg most for *rags;* our house being new, we
have none.   I am tolerably well, and cannot be too
thankful for good nerves.   Louis is very low at
times, nervous at leaving me; and for him I keep
up, though at times not without a struggle.   May
the Almighty watch over us, and not separate us, is
my hourly prayer!

In your hands we feel the children so safe,
though we miss them much.   It is so kind of you
to have taken them, and they are strong and
healthy. . . .

June 25.

Two words by Lady Ely's courier.   I am so glad
she is here.   She performed the journey in a day
and night without difficulty; and Christa, who
merely came from Cassel, took three days coming
by road.

Alas! to-morrow Louis' division moves on into
the country to make room for other troops, and he
must go.   It will be too far for him to return—save
with special permission for a few hours—so we shall

have to part. My courage is beginning to fail me, but I bear up as best I can. God knows what a bitter trial it is! He is just in front, so the first exposed. William is to go in Uncle Alex's staff, and my poor mama-in-law is beginning to break down now. We try to cheer each other. The whole thing is so hard: against her countrymen—there where Louis has served. The whole thing is so *contre-cœur*, and the Prussian soldiers dislike it as much as we do.

I am going to Frankfort with ever so many poor wives to take leave of their husbands, who march to-day.

The heat is awful. I have no time to think of myself, or I dare say I should have heat, &c., to complain of. Being still off and on with Louis, and having things to do, keeps me up; but when he is gone, and I have no man here to reassure me, it will be dreadful.

I must close. . . . Letters from home *now* are such a pleasure; do let anyone write to me sometimes to give me news of you all.

Your own child,

ALICE.

Darmstadt: July 1.

. . . The parting *now* was *so* hard! and he feels it so dreadfully. I can scarcely manage to write. The heat, besides, is overpowering. Our dear wedding-day four years ago! Four years of undisturbed, real, and increasing happiness. How I thank and bless the Almighty for them, and how fervently I pray that we may live over this most bitter trial!

. . . Whether Henry is engaged or not we don't know, and can get no news of him. At any rate he is cut off from news of us and the rest of Germany; and, as our army is moving, and he is on the extreme wing, at any moment he may find himself opposite to his own brothers and countrymen. It is most painful, and has been to my poor father-in-law a great shock, as we all hoped he had got away. Please let my brothers know this. They will feel for this unheard-of position for three brothers to be in. . . .

Dear Lady Ely is a comfort and support to me, and it was quite a relief to Louis to leave her with me. We are both so grateful that she came. Christa is quite out of sorts about her country, and sees everything black. Marie is low about her brother; and we are so in the middle of it all, that an

English person who has no one concerned in it all
is really a relief.

I am so glad that you are pleased with the
little ones. You will be sure, I know, not to let
them get in the way of infection, if there is still
any.

July 3.

. . . Poor Vicky! She bears her trial [the
death of her son, Prince Sigismund] bravely, and
it is a heavy one indeed. This dreadful war is
enough to break one's heart. Those lives sacrificed
for nothing—and what will be the end of it all?
All our troops are gone now, too, and, what is so
unpleasant, of course we here don't know where
they go to—where they are. Letters are fetched
by the Feldpost, and as they are chiefly not near
the railroads—at least not Louis—we cannot telegraph. At such a moment I know dear Louis
fidgets dreadfully for news, and I not less. Since
he has gone I have heard nothing.

I am so very uncomfortable, and it wants
courage and patience and hope, under such circumstances, to bear all. Of course anxiety about beloved Louis is the chief thing, and longing for
news. The Prussians are collecting a large army
near Thüringen, in which direction ours are march-

ing. Probably Uncle Ernest against ours! He might so well have remained quiet, and sent his troops to Mayence, as was settled.

For dear Lenchen's wedding-day receive every warm and affectionate wish. May God's blessing rest on their union! I am so glad you are pleased with the dear children. I have already found that likeness in Ella to Affie's picture by Thorburn, but she is so like dear Louis.

July 6.

. . . There seems a chance of an armistice. * I trust it is so, and that peace will ensue. The enormous bloodshed on both sides this fortnight is too awful to think of. ** Poor Austria! it is hard for her. But as she is said to be ready to cede Venice, then at least the Italian war will be at an end.

Surely the neutral Powers will try and prevent Austria and Prussia beginning again; it is too horrid!

* An armistice of five days was agreed upon on July 22.

** On June 27, the Austrians had been defeated after a stubborn fight at Nachod, with a loss of over six thousand men killed. Other battles took place within a few days at Podoll, Münchengrätz, and Trautenau. On July 3 was fought the decisive battle of Sadowa, in which the Austrians are said to have lost nearly forty thousand men.

The rest of Germany now must knock under; but that is better than again shedding so much blood on the chance of getting the upper hand.

I have had some lines from dear Louis from the north of Hesse. He is well; how I do hope now that they won't come to blows.

How kind of you to give the children frocks for the wedding! Will you kiss the dear little ones from me? I miss them very much.

Darmstadt: July 19.

Beloved Mama,

What a time I have passed during these eight days since Baby's birth!* Firstly, I have to thank the Almighty for having preserved my own sweet and adored husband, and for the blessing of having had him by me, so dear, so precious, during my confinement. After three days he had to go, and when he got near Aschaffenburg found fighting going on.** We could hear the guns here. The Prussians shot from the roofs of the houses; they fought in the streets; it must have been horrid.

---

* Irène, born July 12, 1866.
** On July 14 the German Federal troops were defeated at Aschaffenburg.

Our troops retreated (as had always been intended) in perfect order. The wounded were brought in here the following day. The 13th and 14th they fought. Louis was there on the 14th; since then I have not seen him—God knows when I shall again.

The Prussians have taken Frankfort, and they are at home here. No communications allowed; get no papers or letters; may send none! An existence of monstrous anxiety and worry, which it is impossible for those to imagine who have not lived through it.

I had a letter from Louis from the Odenwald this morning, written yesterday. They expected to pass Amorbach to-day. They are trying to meet the Bavarians, who are never to be found.

I long for a letter from you. We have none at all, and I have had none from you since Baby's birth. The people, who are such cowards and so silly, fly from here in all available droschkies.

How I pray some end may soon come to this horrid bloodshed! Ah! the misery around us you can't imagine. Henry has never received his discharge, and has gone unscathed, in spite of being so exposed through all these battles.

I myself am very well, and I don't give way,

though the anxiety about Louis leaves me no peace.

Baby is well and very pretty. The time she came at prevented a thought of disappointment at her being a girl. Only gratitude to the Almighty filled our hearts, that I and the child were well, and that dear Louis and I were together at the time. The times are hard; it wants all a Christian's courage and patience to carry one through them; but there is *one Friend* who in the time of need does not forsake one, and He is my comfort and support. God bless you, my own Mama, and pray for your child,

ALICE.

Friday, July 27, 9 o'clock P.M.

At this moment the messenger has arrived, to leave again at five to-morrow morning. A thousand thanks for your dear letter, the first I have received since Baby's birth!

To-night (since Sunday no news of Louis) at length I have heard that dear Louis is well. These last four days they have been fighting again. I had a few lines from him. These last two nights he slept in a field, and the country is so poor that they had nothing but a little bread during two

days to eat. Now the Prussians, having made peace
with Austria, and having refused it to us, are ad-
vancing on our troops from three sides.

I can scarcely write; this anxiety is killing me,
and my love has been so exposed! All are in admiration of his personal bravery and tender attention to the suffering and want of all around. He
never thinks of himself, and shares all the dangers
and privations with the others.

Louis says they long for peace. He disapproves
the different Governments for not now giving way
to Prussia, and begs me to use my influence with
Uncle Louis to accept Prussian conditions to spare
further bloodshed.

From all parts of the country the people beg me
to do what I can.

The confusion here is awful, the want of money
alarming; right and left one must help. As the
Prussians pillaged here, I have many people's things
hidden in the house. Even whilst in bed I had to
see gentlemen in my room, as there were things to
be done and asked which had to come straight to
me. Then our poor wounded — the wives and
mothers begging I should inquire for their husbands
and children. It is a state of affairs too dreadful
to describe.

The new anxiety to-night of knowing a dreadful

battle is expected, perhaps going on, in which dear
Louis again must be! I can scarcely bear up any
longer; I feel it is getting too much. God Almighty
stand by us! My courage is beginning to sink. I
see no light anywhere; and my own beloved husband still in danger, and we cannot hear, for the
Prussians are between us and them. Anything
may have happened to him, and I can't hear
it or know it! I could not go to him were he
wounded.

What I have suffered and do suffer no words
can describe—the sleepless nights of anxiety, the
long days without news—*how* I pray it may soon
end, and dear darling Louis be spared me!

In these days I have so longed to hear from
you. It would have been such a comfort, and I
longed for it much.

If we live, and peace is restored, the country
and everything will be in such a mess, and both of
us in such want of change, that we must go somewhere; but we shall then, I fear, be next to ruined.
You can't think what war in one's own country—in
a little one like this—is! The want is fearful. I
must go to bed, as it is late. I am well, so is the
little one; but I can't sleep or eat well all along;
and the worry of mind and much to do keep me
weak.

15*

Oh, that we were together again! Good-bye, beloved Mama. These next days I fear will be dreadful. May the Almighty watch over dear Louis! You will pray for him, won't you?

P.S.—The standard of Louis' cavalry regiment, which they did not take with them, and which is usually kept at the Schloss, is in my room for safety.

Forgive the shocking writing, but I am so upset to-night, since my messenger of Tuesday returned with Louis' letter.

Darmstadt: August 4.

. . . The linen, &c., for the wounded has arrived, and been so useful; a thousand thanks for it! Matters here change from one day to another and I hope Louis may soon be able to return with the troops. Uncle Louis I do hope and pray will then return, and I hope he will regain the favour which he had lost, for any change now would be dreadful.

My father-in-law is really in such a state since these events, and his nerves so shattered, that my mother-in-law trembles for him, and tries to keep him out of all. He is so angry, so heartbroken at the loss of Oberhessen, which is probable, that he wishes not to outlive it. My poor mama-in-law burst into tears this morning in my room, where this scene took place.

I have just returned from having been to enquire after the wounded at the different hospitals and houses, which are filling fast, as they can be brought from Aschaffenburg, Laufach, &c. As soon as I am better, I will go to them myself; but the close and crowded wards turn one easily faint.

Becker saw Louis three days ago, and accompanied him to Munich for a day. I hear he is well, though for six nights he had slept out of doors, and the last three nights it had poured incessantly; and all that time—on account of ours not having a truce, and expecting to be attacked—they were, being such a mass together, without provisions, barely a morsel of bread. I am so distressed about poor Anton Hohenzollern* and Obernitz; so many acquaintances and friends have fallen on both sides, it is dreadful!

The town is full of Prussians. I hope they will not remain too long, for they pay for nothing, and the poor inhabitants suffer so much. There is cholera in the Prussian army, and one soldier lies here ill of it. I hope it won't spread.

* Prince Anton Hohenzollern, son of Prince Hohenzollern. He died from diphtheria in a hospital, the result of a wound received during the war.

August 13.

. . . It is fearful. Those who have seen the
misery war brings with it, near by—the sufferings,
the horror—know well what a scourge it is. May
the Almighty spare our poor Germany this new evil!
I forgot to thank you in Louis' name, as he had
told me, for your letter, which he found here on his
return. He is to-day still at Berlin, and we are so
grateful for your having written to good Fritz.
What he can do I know he will.

Uncle Louis is still at Munich, and I don't think
he will abdicate; besides, he is at this moment
doing what his country wishes.

I received a letter from Julie Battenberg,* saying what Uncle Alexander had written to her about
Louis: "Le Prince Alexandre m'écrit qu'il a obtenu
du Grand Duc la démission de Perglas" (who commanded the troops so badly), "et la nomination du
Prince Louis en commandement de nos troupes; il
me dit à cette occasion que votre Mari pendant
cette triste campagne s'est fait aimer et apprécier
de tout le monde, qu'il s'est fait une excellente
réputation, et qu'il sera reçu à bras ouverts par la
troupe." . . . It is a large command for one so
young, and with so little experience—all the more

* Princess Battenberg, wife of Prince Alexander of Hesse.

so, as we don't know how long peace may last. He
is sent to Berlin, as the country all look to Louis to
prevent new evil; and all this without poor Louis
having any direct position of heir to be able to en-
force his opinion. He has no easy life of it.

The horse you gave Louis he rode in the different engagements, and praised him very much.
He stood the fire quite well, but not the bursting of
the shells close by.

About the children, the 23rd is quite soon
enough for their departure.

We shall not call baby "Irène," unless all seems
really peaceful, and at this moment it does not
look promising. I am very sad and dismayed at
the whole look-out. My mother-in-law was so pleased
with your letter, and thanks you warmly for it.

Nierstein, Gelbes Haus: August 17.

This dear day makes me think so much of you,
of home, and of those two dear ones whose memories are so precious, and who live on with us,
and make me often think that we had parted only
yesterday.

We are so pleased at your saying that you claim
Louis as *your* son. He always considers *himself* in
particular your child, and if anything helps to
stimulate him in doing his duty well, it is the sin-

cere wish of being worthy to claim and deserve
that title. Darling Papa would be proud of him,
and pleased to see how earnestly he takes his
duties, and how conscientiously and unselfishly he
fulfils them, for he has had and still has many
trials—things I can tell you of when we meet again.

Life is such a pilgrimage, and so uncertain is
its duration, that all minor troubles are forgotten
and easily borne, when one thinks what one must
live for.

Before leaving Darmstadt yesterday to come here,
we went to see some of the wounded again. One
poor man had died since I was last there: he had
been so patient, and had suffered so much. Another had had an operation performed and was very
low—he was crying like a child. I could scarcely
comfort him; he held my hand and always moaned
out "Es brennt so" [It burns so]. Such nice people
most of those young men are—very young, and for
that class so well educated. All who are well enough
are reading.

I must praise the ventilation and cleanliness in
the different hospitals; in these things they have
made wonderful progress here.

We are here in Rheinhessen, as Louis has to
take his command. This place, Nierstein, lies between Worms and Mayence, and all our troops are

quartered about here. Louis' staff is at Worms, where he himself is to-day, and was already last night.

He was more hopeful about the prospects for Oberhessen on his return from Berlin, and had been so kindly received by dear Vicky and Fritz.

When Louis wrote his Farewell to his cavalry brigade (who are so sorry to lose him), as a remembrance that he and they had stood in the field together for their first campaign, he asked these two regiments, officers and men, to stand sponsors to Baby, as she was born during that time, and they are delighted, but wish the child to have one of their names! We wait till the troops can come home to christen Baby, on that account. . . . I don't think we shall be here very long. Whenever the Prussians leave Darmstadt, we can return.

Nierstein, Gelbes Haus: August 21.

. . . We are here still, and all our troops, and Louis has a great deal to do. To-morrow the armistice is over, and at present we have no news as to its prolongation or the settlement of peace; but it must be one or other. A little private war of Prussia against us would be absurd and impossible, so the troops remain quartered in the different villages about here. The country here is so rich and fertile, the villages so clean, with such good houses; but the people are blessed with children to an extraordinary extent! It is the most richly populated part of all Germany, and there are more people on the square mile than in England.

The change of air—though it is but two hours from Darmstadt—has done me good, and if later, through your great kindness, a little journey should be possible to us, it would be very beneficial to both of us.

This house is quite close to the Rhine, and this instant our pioneers have come by from Worms on their pontoon bridge singing a quartett, about twenty or thirty men. It looks so pretty, and they sing so beautifully. On their marches the soldiers always sing, and they have so many beautiful songs, such as: "Der gute Kamerad." The Germans are such a *gemüthlich* [simple, kindly, sociable] people. The more one lives with them, the more one learns to appreciate them. It is a fine nation. God grant this war, which has produced so many heroes, and cost so many gallant lives, may not have been in vain, and that at length Germany may become a mighty, powerful Power! It will then be the first in the world, where the great ideas and thoughts come from, free from narrow-minded prejudice, and when once the Germans have attained political freedom, they will be lastingly happy and united.

But the present state of things is sad, though one should not despair of some good resulting from it.

My letter is quite confused. I beg a thousand pardons for it, but I have been interrupted so often.

Gelbes Haus: August 29.

... The children arrived well and safe, and in such good looks. It was a great pleasure to see them again; and I tried to make Victoria tell me as much as possible of dear Grandma and uncles and aunts, and when she is not absent-minded she is very communicative. How much we thank you, darling Mama, for having kept them and been so good to them, I can't tell you. This change has been so good for them; for now there are both cholera and small-pox at Darmstadt, which is still full of Prussian soldiers. More have come, and our peace is not yet concluded. I hope it is no bad sign, and that the hopes of losing less will not disappear.

We were only in Darmstadt for the day when the children arrived, and we go there for a few hours to-morrow on business. Louis has a great deal to do, and all the military things are in his hands.

I am not feeling very well. The air here after a few days is relaxing, and I begin to feel more what a strain there has been on my nerves during this time. I have such a pain in my side again. Mountain air Weber wants me to have, and quiet, away from all bothers; but I fear that is impossible *now*, on account of Louis not being able to leave— and then financially.

I have some *Heimweh* [home-sickness] after dear England, Balmoral, and all at home, I own, though the joy of being near dear Louis again is *so* great! But life is meant for work, and not for pleasure, and I learn more and more to be grateful and content with that which the Almighty sends me, and to find the sunshine in spite of the clouds; for when one has one's beloved, adored husband by one's side, what is there in the world that is too heavy to bear? My own darling Mama, when I think of darling Papa and of you, and that he is not *visible* at your side now, I long to clasp you to my heart, in some way to cheer the loneliness which is a poor widow's lot. Oh, none in the world is harder than that!

Darmstadt: August 31.

... Thank you for telling me how you spent
that dear day; it must have been peaceful and
solemn, the beautiful country harmonising well with
the thoughts of that great and beautiful soul which
ever lives on with us. He remains nearer and
nearer to me, and the recollection of many things
dear Papa told me is a help and a stay in my ac-
tions, particularly of late. The separation seems so
short. I can see him and hear him speak so plainly.
Alas! my children have never seen him. Through
you, darling Mama, and in your rooms, and at your
side, they must learn to know him, that they may
become worthy of their descent.

Yesterday we saw the children. Victoria is not
quite well, but Ella is well, and won't leave me
when I come into the room; she keeps kissing me
and putting her fat arms round my neck. There is
each time a scene when I go away. She is so affectionate: so is dear Victoria. I send you a photograph of our smallest, who is such a pretty child,
and very good.

The peace is not concluded yet; more Prussians
have been quartered in and around Darmstadt.
The people are very angry at this lasting so long....
They believe it is *Strafeinquartierung* [done to
punish us]. Nothing is settled as to what we keep

or lose, and we know and hear nothing. Waiting here, uncomfortably lodged, the troops impatient to go home, as they have nothing to do, gets very irksome.

Gelbes Haus: September 8.

. . . At last the peace is concluded, though not yet ratified. The terms are not so bad. We lose the Hinterland and the Domains there, as also the whole of Hesse-Homburg—in all sixty-four thousand souls—pay three millions contribution, besides having kept a large part of the Prussian army six weeks for nothing, which cost the country twenty-five thousand florins daily. For Oberhessen we go into the North-German Bund, and half the army is under Prussian command, which will make a dreadful confusion. Louis would prefer having it for the whole, particularly in anticipation, alas! of a coming war.

The railroads, posts, and telegraphs also become Prussian; and they demand, besides, some fine old pictures, books, and manuscripts, which had once belonged to the Kölner Dom, and were made a present of to this country years ago; and for our Domains no *Entschädigung* [compensation]. In exchange for Homburg we get some small places—amongst others, Rumpenheim.

When the peace is ratified and the money paid, the Prussians leave the country, which must now be very shortly. Until then Louis must stop here, and as he can only get leave now and then to go to Darmstadt, and that always uncertain, Baby's christening is still impossible, as Louis must be there. She will be called "Irène Louise Marie Anna."

Gelbes Haus: September 11.

. . . Tired of constantly putting off and waiting, we settled yesterday to have Baby christened to-morrow, as it is Louis' birthday, and to go for the day to Darmstadt. Though the Prussians are still there, some of the godfathers are coming over, otherwise it will be quite quiet.

. . . How true and sad is what you say, dear Mama, about life and its trials! Alas! that it should be you, dear loving kind Mama, who have had to drink so deeply of that cup of bitterness! Those who possess all they love, as I do, can, however, feel all the more keenly, and sympathise more truly with you for what you have lost, though it is a grief we do not know. How I do long always to alleviate this grief for you, dearest Mama; but that is the world's trial. None can bear the burden for you. One must carry it oneself; and it wants patience and courage to bear such as yours, dear

Mama. I feel for you now more than ever since during that month I feared from day to day my happy life might be brought to a violent close, and anticipated all the misery that *might* come, but which the Almighty graciously averted.

Darmstadt: September 16.

The name Irène,* through other associations, is one my parents-in-law and we like; it stands, besides, as a sort of recollection of the peace so longed for, and which I so gladly welcomed. It will always remind us of the time, and of how much we have to be grateful for.

Darmstadt: September 24.

. . . We are settled here again; our troops have returned and Uncle Louis likewise. The former were received most warmly by the inhabitants and showered with nosegays—Louis also, who rode at their head. We saw them all in front of the Schloss, and it was sad to see the thinned ranks and to miss the absent faces we knew so well. On the 13th and 14th of July at Frohnhofen, Laufach, and Aschaffenburg, out of 8,000 we lost 800 men and

---

* The Princess Charles had a sister, who died when a child, who had borne that name.

11 officers, and of the officers just those who were very intimate with the Prussians, and who wished Germany to be united under Prussia.

This afternoon we are going to see after the poor wounded, some of whom are still very ill with such horrible wounds. So much suffering and pain and grief to those poor people, who are innocent in this unhappy war!

If only now the other sovereigns will forget their antipathies and the wrongs they have suffered from Prussia, and think of the real welfare of their people and the universal fatherland, and make those sacrifices which will be necessary to prevent the recurrence of these misfortunes!

The poor Homburgers marched by with our troops, and their tears and ours fell as we saw them (who had fought so bravely under Uncle Louis) for the last time before they become Prussians, and return to their homes as such.

October 1.

. . . I can but write a few lines, as we are going with the children to Uncle Alexander to Jugenheim for a few days. The change of air is wanted for Ella, who is still pale; and Irène has never had any change yet, and is also rather pale.

We were at Frohnhofen and Laufach a few days

ago to see where the unfortunate engagement was, and visited the graves of our soldiers. In the middle of a field there is a mound, below which some eighty men and some officers lie, and so on. It makes a very sad impression, for as our troops retreated, and they were buried by the people, none know which of the common soldiers or even which of the officers lie in the different places. We found some balls, and things the soldiers had thrown off during the fight. In one grave in the churchyard, the wounded who died afterwards are buried. I asked who lay there, and the gravedigger answered, "Ein Preuss' und ein Hess' liegen dort beisammen" ["A Prussian and a Hessian lie there together"], united in death, and fallen by each other's hand, perhaps. Some of the officers who accompanied us, and had not been there since the engagement, were much overcome on seeing the graves of their comrades. I put wreaths and flowers on them, and ordered crosses where we knew who lay there.

The wounded here are recovering, and I go often to see after them.

As you say, this large Prussia is by no means an united Germany; but, nevertheless, I think the duty of the other German sovereigns, in spite of all, is to unite with Prussia and place themselves under her, so as to make her unite with Germany.

Otherwise, the next opportunity, they will be annexed.

Darmstadt: October 22.

On Thursday we are going to Waldleiningen for a fortnight and take Victoria with us. The two little girls knew your photograph at once, and began, of course, to talk of you and of England.

Waldleiningen: October 31.

. . . It is quite beautiful here. We found dear Ernest, Marie * and children well; the former so kind and dear, as they always are. Victoria and Alberta ** get on tolerably together. The little boy is splendid, so strong and fat.

The Castle is so fine and lies just in the midst of mountains and woods, and there are walks without end—many of them reminding me so much of Scotland.

The Nichels came to see us, and Marie and I played with Nichel; *** it reminded me so much of the good old times to see him.

Ella's birthday is to be kept when we return.

---

* Prince and Princess Leiningen.
** Princess Alberta of Leiningen.
*** Formerly one of the Royal Band in England. Madame Nichel had been a dresser of the Duchess of Kent's.

16*

She is too small to know the difference of the day.
I thank you beforehand for the locket for her with
dear Papa's picture. The children always speak of
their two Grandpapas—dear Grandpapa in Heaven,
and dear Grandpapa in Darmstadt. Victoria, hearing Papa so often mentioned, and seeing his pictures
about everywhere, asks no end of questions about
him.

Darmstadt: November 14.

I am better, thank you, but I am so weak without the least reason, and dreadfully chilly. Still, I
go out regularly in all weathers and take exercise,
but of an evening I am quite knocked up.

We always breakfast at half-past eight, as Louis
gets up early and prefers it; so that I lead a very
healthy life, and in spite of that am not well. A
change quite into another climate for a few months
was what I really required; but it was impossible.
On that account, dear Mama, I shall hope to have
a full three months in England when we come, and
perhaps part of the time with Bertie, if he can have
us. I went through a great deal this summer during
my confinement. The excitement and the will to
keep well kept me so at the time, but I feel it now,
alas! and show it, too, for I am getting so thin
again.

November 22.

A thousand thanks for the precious book,* and for your dear lines. The former I have nearly finished. I got it yesterday morning, and you can well imagine that every spare moment was devoted to its study.

I think it very well done, and I am only sorry that General Grey cannot continue it, as the other persons, I believe, did not know dear Papa. The longer I live, the more I see and know of the world, the deeper my tender admiration grows for such a father. It makes me feel myself so small, so imperfect, when I think that I am his child, and am still so unworthy of being it. How many people here who like to hear of dear Papa ask me about him, and you can understand with what pride and love I talk of him, and tell them things which make them all share our sorrow at not having him here any more! But if ever a life has outlived a man, dear Papa's has done so. In my thoughts and aims he ever remains the centre and the guiding star. Dear beloved Papa, he never half knew how much, even when a foolish child, I loved and adored him. His great life will be a model for many and many

* *The Early Years of the Prince Consort*, by the late General Grey.

for generations to come, and his great thoughts and aims can leave none idle who knew them.

You kindly 'ask how I am. Better, thank you, since I have begun some bark—quinine I can't take, or else I should have been well sooner.

Victoria I am teaching to read—in playing with cards with different letters on them.

November 30.

To-day it is six whole years since we were engaged to each other in the Red Drawing-room at Windsor, when we in dear Papa's little room after-wards received your and dear Papa's sanction to it. And the following year—how sad that already was, for darling Papa was beginning to be unwell! How constantly do I think of you, beloved Mama, during that fortnight of anxiety and sorrow! God merci-fully spared you to us, though for yourself it was the commencement of the sad and lonely existence you lead without dear Papa.

I am sure it is good for little Henry* to be this winter with you in England: the Berlin climate is very unwholesome. Health is such a blessing. If one has children, the first wish is they should be healthy, for ill health influences all, and nothing more than temper.

* Son of the Crown Prince and Princess of Prussia.

We intend, if possible, going for a day or two to Carlsruhe. Poor Louise and Fritz went through so much that is painful this summer. . . .

I read an immense deal now of serious, and what some call dry, books; but it is a great resource to me, and the thought of standing still, if one does not study, urges me on. The long winter evenings we always spend together, and twice in the week receive in the evening, when I play on the piano duets with such as play on the violin, and pass the evenings very pleasantly.

Carlsruhe: December 6.

Thousand thanks for your dear letter! I congratulate you on all having gone off so well at Wolverhampton,* and am very grateful for the account. Dear Bertie's visit is over, and it has been a very great pleasure to us to have seen him again, and to have him under our own roof—where we at length had an opportunity, in a small way, to return his hospitality and constant kindness to us. God bless him, dear brother! he is the one who has from my childhood been so dear to me.

We have come here, and I think it has pleased

---

* The uncovering of the monument to the Prince Consort.

good Fritz. Louis seems very well. I saw Lady
Fanny Baillie yesterday, looking dear and pretty as
ever. It is a pleasure to look at her sweet face.

Carlsruhe: December 11.

As every year during *these days* my thoughts are
with you, and as each year brings round again the
anniversary of that dreadful misfortune, it seems
more and more impossible that five years should
already have elapsed, since He whom we all loved
so tenderly was taken from our sight. How I thank
the Almighty again and again, as this season returns,
that He spared you to us, when at such a moment
we trembled for your precious life, fearing that two
so united in life even in death could not be parted!
What should we poor children, what would the
country have done, had that second misfortune
come over us! Yet it seemed selfish and unkind
to wish for your loving wife's heart the solitary
widow's existence. How bravely and nobly you
have borne it!

Now I must end, beloved Mama. God bless you
and comfort you, and in these days let sometimes
the thought of your absent child, who was at your
side during that dreadful time, mingle with the recollection of the past!

Darmstadt: December 14.

Beloved, precious Mama,

On awaking this morning, my first thoughts were of you and of dear darling Papa! Oh, how it re-opens the wounds scarcely healed, when this day of pain and anguish returns! This season of the year, the leafless trees, the cold light, everything reminds me of that time!

Thousand thanks for your dear letter received yesterday. *Well*, only *too well*, do I remember every hour, almost every minute, of those days, and I have such an inexpressible longing to throw my arms round your neck, and to let my tears flow with yours, while kneeling at that beautiful grave.

The tender love and the deep sorrow caused by His loss remain ever with me, and will accompany me through life. At the age I then was, with its sensitive feelings, it made an impression which, I think, nothing can efface—above all, the witnessing your grief. Happily married as I am, and with such a good, excellent and loving husband, how far more can I understand *now* the depth of that grief, which tore your lives asunder! I played our dear Papa's organ under his beloved picture this morning, and my heart and my thoughts were in dear England with you all.

We found our children well on our return, and
Irène prospers perfectly on her donkey's milk.

My mother-in-law is so much pleased with the
book,* and it has interested her very much. She
came to see me early this morning on account of
its being the 14th. She is always so kind and full
of attentions.

Darmstadt: December 21.

. . . I hope by this time that you are quite recovered, though this mild damp weather is not
made to give one strength. I feel it so much also,
and am really only kept alive by steel, for off and
on I am so weak, that I nearly faint if I have to
stand any time, and this is so unpleasant.

. . . I am trying to found what is no small undertaking: a "Frauenverein," to be spread all over the
land in different committees, the central one being
here under my direction, for the purpose of assisting
the International Convention for nursing and supporting the troops in time of war, which was founded
at Geneva, and to which this country also belongs.
The duty in time of peace will be to have nurses
brought up and educated for the task, who can
then assist in other hospitals or amongst the poor,

* General Grey's *Early Years of the Prince Consort.*

or to nurse the rich, wherever they may be required. In time of war this committee of women has to collect all the necessary things for the wounded and for the marching troops, has to see to their being sent to right places, &c.

All these things were done by private people in this war, and, though quantities of things were sent, the whole plan was not organised, so that there was want and surplus at the same time.

In time of peace these things should be organised, so that, when war comes, people know where to send their things to, and that no volunteer nurses go out who have not first learnt their business.

The same thing exists in Baden, in Bavaria, and in Prussia, and here it is much wanted. But all these undertakings are difficult, particularly in the choice of persons to assist one. Still I hope I shall be able to do it. My mother-in-law helps me, and I hope before long to be able to begin.

The Elector is coming here on a visit to-day, and Uncle Alexander returned from Petersburg last night.

Darmstadt: December 30.

. . . May the Almighty give you every blessing of peace and comfort which the world can still give you, till you gain that greater blessing and reward above all others, which is reserved for such as my own sweet mother! May every blessing fall on my old dear home, with all its dear ones! May peace, and the glory which peace and order bring with it, with its many blessings, protect my native land; and may, in the new year, your wise and glorious reign, so overshadowed by dear Papa's spirit, continue to prosper and be a model and an ornament to the world!

This year of pain and anxiety, and yet for us so rich in blessings, draws to a close. It moves me more than ever as its last day approaches. For how much have we not to thank the Almighty—for my life, which is so unworthy compared to many others, the new life of this little one, and above all the preservation of my own dear husband, who is my all in this life!

The trials of this year must have brought some good with all the evil: good to the individual and good to the multitude. God grant we may all profit by what we have learnt, and gain more and more that trust in God's justice and love, which is our guide and support in trouble and in joy! Oh, more than ever have I felt in this year, that God's goodness and love are indeed beyond comprehension!

. . . I am really glad to hear that you can listen

to a little music. Music is such a heavenly thing, and dear Papa loved it so much, that I can't but think that now it must be soothing, and bring you near to him. . . .

1867.

Gotha: January 15.

I am delighted to hear of dear Arthur having passed so good an examination. How proud you must be of him! And the good Major,* who has spared no pains, I know—how pleased he must be! Arthur has a uniform now, I suppose.

Berlin: January 26.

. . . We remain here a little longer, probably until the following Saturday, as the King, owing to his cold, could not see us often, and begged us to remain longer.

I saw Amalie Lauchert ** here two days ago, looking so well and charming as ever.

* Major Elphinstone, Prince Arthur's Governor from 1859, now Sir Howard Elphinstone, K.C.B.

** Princess Amalie of Hohenlohe-Schillingsfürst, niece of Queen Victoria's late brother-in-law, Prince of Hohenlohe-Langenburg, married to an artist, Herr Lauchert.

Little Vicky is such a darling, very like her poor little brother—so merry, so good, one never hears her cry—and it is really a comfort to Vicky to have that dear little thing. Poor Vicky is very sad and low at times.

After intense cold it is quite warm, like spring, which is very unwholesome and tiring.

Darmstadt: February 16.

. . . I think I can understand what you must feel. I know well what those first three years were —what fearful suffering, tearing and uprooting those feelings which had been centred in beloved Papa's existence! It is indeed, as you say, "in mercy," that after the long storm a lull and calm ensues, though the violent pain, which is but the reverse side of the violent love, seems only to die out with it, and that is likewise bitter. Yet, beloved Mama, could it be otherwise? There would be no justice or mercy, were the first stage of sorrow to be the perpetual one; and God grant, that time may still soothe and alleviate that which it cannot change! I can only imagine what the loss must be, if I measure it by the possession of that one adored being, who is the centre and essence of my existence.

Darmstadt: February 28.

. . . Yesterday we had a very interesting lecture in our house about Art in Venice, by a young Swede [Herr von Molin], who has been studying three years in Italy. We had the room full of people, artists and professors, who liked to listen.

. . . All the natural cleverness and sharpness in the world won't serve nowadays, unless one has learnt something. I feel this so much; and just in our position it is more and more required and expected, particularly in a small place, where so much depends on the personal knowledge and exertions of the Princes.

Darmstadt: April 1.

. . . I could not write the other day, as I had a good deal to do with two committees for charities, which had to be got into order, and which took up a great deal of my time.

Cold, hail, snow, and rain have returned; and Irène has got a cold, which most people here have. The weather is so unpleasant.

We shall stop here in town until we go to England, as we have nowhere to go to before. It is a pity for the children to have no country air, and they miss the flowers in their walks. I can't

praise Orchard* enough.   Such order she keeps,
and is so industrious and tidy, besides understanding so much about the management of the children's
health and characters.

Darmstadt: April 5.

Thousand thanks for your dear letter, and for
the kind wishes for Victoria's birthday!   I pray she
may be a worthy granddaughter of my darling
Mama!   I shall never forget that day—your kindness to us, and the tender nurse you were. . . .

Victoria means to dictate a letter to you; she is
so much pleased with her presents.   Irène has not
a tooth yet, and is not very fat, poor little thing!
but she is fresh and rosy, and, I think, strong.

This last week the excitement here has been
dreadful, as all anticipated a war with France on
account of Luxemburg.   I fear sooner or later it
will come.   May the Almighty avert such a calamity!

The Moriers were quite in ecstasies about your
handsome present.   The christening** went off
very well.

---

* Their nurse, who is still with the youngest child, Princess
Alix.

** Of their child, to whom Queen Victoria stood sponsor.

April 8.

. . . We have just returned from church, and
to-morrow morning we all take the Sacrament at
nine o'clock in the Schlosskirche. Professor Jowett
is here on a visit to the Moriers, and is going to
read the service on Sunday. I have not had an
opportunity to attend our English service since we
were at Windsor, excepting one Sunday at Berlin
with Vicky and Fritz.

People think now, the evil of war is put off for
a few weeks, but that is all. Henry is here for
Easter, and says the same from all he heard at
Berlin.

April 21.

. . . How I wish you may be right in *not* be-
lieving in war! I always fear it is not Luxemburg,
but the intense jealousy of the French nation, that
they should not be the first on the Continent, and
that Germany is becoming independent and power-
ful against their will. Then, again, the Germans
feel their new position, and assert their rights with
more force because unanimous, and neither nation
will choose to give in to the other.

The war would be totally useless, and sow no
end of dissension and hatred between the two neigh-
bour countries, who, for their own good as for that

of mankind, ought to live in peace and harmony with each other.

We seem drifting back to the Middle Ages, as each question is pushed to the point of the sword. It is most sad. How dear Papa would have disapproved of much that has happened since 1862!

Is the Catalogue which Mr. Ruland sent some time ago to Mr. Woodward for dear Papa's Raphael Collection in print now?* So many people know of its coming out, and are anxious to see it, as, indeed, I am likewise, for it is the only complete collection in the world, and the world of art is anxious to know all about it. Will you, perhaps, let me know through Mr. Sahl,** as I believe it is already a good while since you approved of its being published, and gave the orders for its being printed?

May 2.

As yet none dare to be sure of the peace, but all live again since there are more chances for its being maintained. But then, I trust it will be a permanent peace, not merely a putting off till next year!

---

* This Catalogue was not completed and made public till 1876.

** Her Majesty's private librarian.

The French press was so very warlike, and it always talks of the French honour not being able to allow such a mighty empire as the German is becoming to gain the upper hand; and then rectification of her frontiers, always wishing for the Rhine.

May 29.

. . . I presided at my committee of seven ladies and four gentlemen a long while yesterday, and to-morrow I have my other one, which is more numerous. It is an easy task, but I hope we shall have good results from our endeavours.

Paris: June 9.

I really am half killed from sight-seeing and fêtes, but all has interested me so much, and the Emperor and Empress [of the French] have been most kind. Yesterday was the ball at the Hôtel de Ville, quite the same as it had been for you and dear Papa, and there were more than 8,000 people there. It was the finest sight I have ever seen, and it interested me all the more, as I knew it was the same as in the year when you were at Paris.

Every morning we went to the Exhibition, and every evening there was a dinner or ball. It was most fatiguing. To-morrow morning we leave, and had really great trouble to get away, for the Emperor and Empress and others begged us so much to remain for the ball at the Tuileries to-morrow night; but we really could not, on account of Wednesday's concert,* as we should barely arrive in time.

The *attentat* on the Emperor of Russia was dreadful, and we were close by at the time. The Empress can't get over it, and she does not leave Uncle Sache's** side for an instant now, and takes him everywhere in her carriage.

To-day we are going with the whole Court to Versailles. Dear Vicky is gone. She was so low the last days, and dislikes going to parties so much just now, that she was longing to get home. The King [of Prussia] wished them both to stop, but only Fritz remained. How sad these days will be for her, poor love! She was in such good looks; everyone here is charmed with her.

Darmstadt: August 4.

We arrived here at midnight on Friday, and I was so knocked up . . . that I was incapable of doing anything yesterday.

* At Buckingham Palace.
** The Emperor of Russia.

. . . My poor Willem was buried yesterday. Everyone regrets the poor child, for he was very dear. I miss him so much here, for he did everything for me, and liked being about me and the children. All our servants went to the burial. It quite upset me here not to find him, for I was really attached to him, and he learnt so well, and was in many ways so nice, though of course troublesome too at times. How short life is, and the instant one is gone, he is so wiped away for others, and one knows *so* absolutely *nothing* about the person any more! Were it not for a strong faith in a future, it would indeed be cruel to bear. No one of the family is here. We leave to-morrow for Zürich, where we shall be at ten at night; the next day to Chur and the next day to St. Moritz.

St. Moritz: August 8.

With perfect weather we accomplished our journey perfectly, and were enchanted with the beautiful scenery from Zürich hither, not to speak of this place.

The first day—5th—we left Darmstadt at 11 A.M., and did not reach Zürich till eleven at night. We got two little rooms in the Hôtel Baur, but the whole place was full. The next morning after break-

fast we went to look at the lovely lake, which is
green and quite transparent. It was a beautiful
warm morning. We left by rail at ten, partly along
the lake of Zürich and then along the Wallenstädter
See, which is long and narrow, with high perpendi-
cular mountains down to the water—very wild and
picturesque. This lake likewise is of that marvellous green colour. We reached Chur at three
that afternoon—a pretty small town, situated close
up against a mountain. We visited a beautiful old
church there, which contains fine old pictures and
relics; it was built in the time of the Romans, and
is still the chief church of the bishopric.

The next morning we two, with Sarah, Logoz
and our footman, left at six o'clock in a diligence
(we both sitting in the coupé in front) with four
horses, for here the road is the grandest one can
imagine, perpetually ascending for two hours, and
then descending again, always along precipices, and
the horses at a quick trot turning sharp round the
corners—which, I assure you, is a trial to the best
nerves. We drove over the Julier Pass, which was
a road already used by the Romans, and which is
almost the highest in Switzerland. One passes close
to the top of the mountains, which have snow on
them, and are wild and rugged like the top of
Lochnagar. Lower down, the mountains are covered

with bright green grass and fir trees, but rocks look out everywhere, and there are constantly lovely waterfalls.

After crossing the Pass, we drove down—very steep, of course nothing on the edge of the road, always zigzag, and at a sharp trot—for some distance down to Silva Plana, where the view over the valley and lakes of the Engadine, where St. Moritz lies, is beyond description beautiful.

We reached this in the evening at six o'clock, the weather being most beautiful. The Curhaus is below the town, and looks like a large asylum. It is overfilled with people. We have two rooms, but our people as yet none, though they hope for some to-morrow.

I saw Dr. Berry, a little Swiss man, and he recommended me to take the baths twice a week, besides drinking the waters; which I have begun this morning at seven o'clock, the usual hour, as one has to walk up and down a quarter of an hour between the glasses. The bath I took at ten. It is tepid and also iron water, which bubbles like soda water, and makes one feel as if insects were crawling over one.

Lina Aumale is here, the Parises and Nemours. Fritz and Louise [of Baden] leave to-morrow. This afternoon we drove with them, in two funny little

"Wägeli" with one horse, to Samaden, where Louise
went into the hotel to see Mme. d'Usedom, who was
lately upset with her carriage off the road, as there
is no barrier, and hurt herself severely. We saw
her brother likewise.

I have sent you a nosegay of Edelweiss and
other Alp flowers. I hope it won't arrive quite dead.
You must fancy them alive, and, if they could speak,
they would tell you how much I love you, and how
constantly I think of you, and of my dear, dear
home!

St. Moritz: August 11.

. . . All the Orleans' left this place suddenly
yesterday, as there are three cases of scarlatina in
the house. We consulted the doctor immediately,
whether he thought it safe for Louis to remain, he
never having had it, and he said "Perfectly, as we
are at the other end of the house, and out nearly
all day."

Victor and Lolo [Count and Countess Gleichen]
are here, and we went out drawing together yesterday; but it is too difficult here. I think constantly
how much you would admire this place: it is indeed
exquisitely beautiful — much the finest scenery I
have ever seen. It is very wild, and reminds me
in parts of dear Scotland.

You say that our home in England is dull now
for those who like to amuse themselves. It is *never*
dull, darling Mama, when one can be with you, for
I have indeed never met a more agreeable charming
companion. Time always flies by, when one is with
you. I hope it is not impertinent my saying so.

St. Moritz: August 13.

. . . . I knew you would feel for me at the loss
of my poor Willem. Of course one must feel that
sort of loss more than that of many a relation, if
one knew the latter but little. I said to Louis at
the time, that Willem's death distressed me more
than would that of several relations who were not
intimate with me. . . .

Yesterday we and the Gleichens went to the
Rosegg Glacier, and to get there had to go from
Pontresina in little *Bergwagen*, which are strong
miniature *Leiterwagen* without springs, and we went
over a horrid path with quantities of stones, so the
shaking was beyond description.

Victor and Lolo go mostly with us, and we always dine together.

I take three glasses beginning at seven in the
morning, and a bath at eight. One lies in a wooden

thing, covered over up to one's chin with boards, and remains so twenty minutes.

We lunch at twelve, and dine at half-past six, and go to bed early. We are out nearly all day long. It is very warm, the sun scorching; my face is quite red-brown, in spite of veils and parasols. I feel already very much better, and Louis says my face is quite fat. I wish we could remain longer than the end of the month, but Louis must be home.

St. Moritz: August 16.

Yesterday we made a beautiful expedition, which it may amuse you to hear of, as in an exaggerated way it reminded me of our nice Scotch ones. The evening before, we left with Victor and Lolo (without servants) about eight o'clock for Pontresina. The country looked more beautiful than ever in the brightest moonlight. We found two very small but clean rooms in an hotel outside the village.

The next morning we got up at half-past four, dressed, and breakfasted, then got on four horses with most uncomfortable saddles, with our guide, Adam Engler, an amusing man, most active and helpful. We saw the sun rising over the snow-covered mountains, and the valleys gradually coming out clearer.

We were to ascend the Piz Languard, a mountain
1,200 feet high. We rode for two hours by a worse
and much steeper road than up the Glassalt, then
walked over rocks, sand, and slippery grass, so steep
that one could not look up to see where one was
going to, quite precipitous on each side, leaving
snow and glacier below us. The last bit has a sort
of immensely high steps hewn in the rock. After
an hour and a half's hard labour we reached the
summit, which is rocky and small—enormous precipices all round. Poor Lolo was giddy for some
time, which was very unpleasant. The view from
the top is most extensive. The Italian, Swiss, and
Tyrolese Alps are all to be seen, but the view was
not very clear. We rested and ate something, and
drank some Lochnagar whisky. The sun was getting intense. We commenced our descent at eleven
o'clock, and had to walk the whole way back, for
one can't ride down. We did not reach Pontresina
till nearly four, as we had to rest several times, our
limbs ached so, for there is no level ground the
whole way, and the stones slip, and it was very hot.
I had quite sore feet with blisters all over, so that
the last hours were really agonising. But it is a
thing to have done, and the view amply repaid
one, though one does not feel tempted to do it a
second time. I feel very well, excepting my face

(which is still burning and quite red), and my unfortunate feet.

St. Moritz: August 21.

. . . Now I will tell you of our expedition. Louis
and I, Victor and Lolo, and a guide, with each a
small bag, left this early on the morning of the 17th
(dear Grandmama's birthday) in a carriage for
Pontresina; from thence, in two of those shaky
Bergwagen, over part of the Bernina Pass, past the
magnificent Morteratsch Glacier, which we saw perfectly. The guide told us he had been there with
Professor Tyndall, and that the latter had observed,
that the glacier advanced a foot a day in the warm
weather, and old people recollect it having been a
mile higher up. We soon left the high-road, and
all vegetation, save grass, for a bad path into the
Val da Fain. The heat was again intense. We
lunched and rested, and then took the horses out of
the carts for us ladies to ride. The scenery was
wild and severe, until we began again to descend,
and came down upon the lovely Livigno Valley,
which is Italian, and covered with brown châlets.
We reached the village of Livigno, with only wooden
huts, by six o'clock, and turned into a funny little
dark inn, in which we four found one small but
clean room for us — most primitive. As the in-

habitants speak a sort of Italian, we had the greatest difficulty to make ourselves understood. Victor cooked part of the dinner, and it was quite good.

We all slept—I resting *on* a bed, the other three on the floor—in this little room, with the small window wide open.

The next morning we left at nine, and drove on no road in such a small carriage—of course, no springs—our husbands at first getting a lift on the horses, without saddles; then on foot up a steep and dangerous ascent. Splendid weather, but too hot. We went over the Pass of the Stretta: a more difficult and rough ground I never crossed in my life, but splendid scenery. We came on a view which was glorious—such enormous snow-covered mountains and glaciers, with the green valleys deep below looking on Italy and the Tyrol.

We reached Bormio by seven, and took up our residence at a bathing-place, quite magnificently situated, very high up—also Italian. The next morning we started early in carriages, and went over the Stelvio Pass. There, nearly at the risk of my neck, I picked for the first time some Edelweiss, which I am very proud of, as it is always difficult and rare to get.

We got down to St. Maria, which is at the upper end of the Münsterthal and belongs to Switzerland.

In the afternoon, dreadfully hot, I was very thirsty
and drank off a glass of milk; but how it tasted! It
was goat's milk; the people keep the cow's milk for
butter and cheese. We remained the night there,
and left the next morning for here, by Zernetz and
Ofen. To get from one valley into another, one
has always to ascend and descend enormous heights,
and always by narrow paths at the edge of precipices. We enjoyed our tour immensely, and got
on perfectly without servants. Packing up my things,
though, every morning was a great trouble, and the
bag would usually not shut at first. The trees growing here are splendid larches and arven;* the latter
grow only in these very high regions and in Siberia.
Victor and his wife are most amiable and pleasant
travelling-companions, and pleased with everything;
not minding to rough it, which we had to do.

Schloss Mainau: August 30.

... We left St. Moritz at seven, and reached
Chur at seven in the evening. The next day we
came on here to Louise of Baden. Fritz is at

---

* A kind of dwarf tree—half pine, half juniper—which
grows in the highest regions of the Alps, and supplies most of
the soft wood used by the Swiss wood-carvers.

Carlsruhe. This place is very lovely, though, alas! the fine mountains are gone, which one always misses so much.

I thought of you more than I can say on the dear 26th, and I felt low and sad all day. Dear Papa! Time has not yet accustomed us to see each anniversary come round again, and he still remain away. It is so inexpressibly hard for you, and you must feel such intense longing for the dear past. There remains a future! that is the only consolation.

To-day we went with Louise by carriage, and then across part of the lake to the property of the Emperor Napoleon, Arenenberg, which the Empress gave him eight years ago, and which was his home with his mother, and where she died. Every picture and bit of furniture is replaced as it was when the Emperor lived there, and he was there himself and replaced everything. It is quite a page in history to see all the things that surrounded the Emperor in the days of his misfortune.

END OF VOL. I.

PRINTING OFFICE OF THE PUBLISHER.

Printed in Great Britain
by Amazon